Dumb Things He Does
Dumb Things She Does

and Just a Few Dumb Things We Both Do!

Holly Wagner

OLIVER NELSON™
THOMAS NELSON PUBLISHERS®
Nashville

A Division of Thomas Nelson, Inc.
www.ThomasNelson.com

Published in Nashville, Tennessee, by Thomas Nelson, Inc.

Library of Congress Cataloging-in-Publication Data

Wagner, Holly.

Dumb things he does, dumb things she does, and just a few dumb things we both do! / Holly Wagner.

p. cm.

ISBN 0-7852-6520-1

1. Marriage. 2. Communication in marriage. 3. Couples. 4. Man-woman relationships. I. Title.

HQ734 .W182 2002

306.81—dc21 2002001357

Printed in Mexico

02 03 04 05 06 QWM 6 5 4 3 2 1

Dedication

This book is dedicated to my readers;
to those of you committed to building
strong marriages in a society
that so desperately needs
to see you succeed.
You can do it!

dumb things he does

Contents

Section 2: Dumb Things We Both Do

Thanks

. . . to my heavenly Father for this awesome life!

. . . to Philip for loving me in spite of the dumb things I do!

. . . to my children, Jordan and Paris, for keeping life exciting!

. . . to my Oasis family for just being family!

. . . to my friends in different parts of the earth for the love and encouragement!

Preface

Remind me that divorce is expensive and murder is against the law!" was a plea I made to a good friend a few years ago. I laugh about that comment now, but back then I wasn't kidding. Not only did it seem that our marriage just wasn't fun anymore, but maintaining it was too much work. Perhaps there have been times when you, too, have felt like that. Perhaps you are feeling like that now! Well, take heart; you are not alone, and there are some answers.

In this book I will present some clear, simple suggestions that certainly helped my marriage and that I believe will help yours. This book is not the ultimate guide to wedded bliss; it does not present all the answers to every problem. This book is just a small piece of the puzzle. There are many books on marriage out there; read some. There are wonderful seminars and conferences available to help us married people; go to one—or more. A great marriage doesn't happen just because you want it; you have to want it enough to learn and grow.

I split this book into three sections: "Dumb Things He Does," "Dumb Things We Both Do," and "Dumb Things She Does." Read whatever section applies to your situation, or read them all. (It's not that big a book!) And after reading, talk. Talk to your spouse about what you've read. Do you agree with this point or that point? Have you done this particular dumb thing? (Let your spouse answer as to whether you have done one of the dumb things!) Remember, marriages are worked out over a lifetime, so relax. Even you—no matter how many dumb things you've done—can strengthen your marriage!

Section 1

dumb things he does

A Note From Holly

I was raised watching *Cinderella,* which in itself isn't bad, but I actually believed in the Prince Charming, happily-ever-after stuff. Imagine my surprise when Philip, my husband, didn't always act like Prince Charming. "Happily ever after" came only after serious work and communication and the laying down of my ego. No, that was definitely not mentioned in the fairy tale.

One of my favorite movies is *Sleepless in Seattle,* and after seeing it, one of my girlfriends remarked that a "part two" would be great. I quickly commented that I wasn't too sure it would be an appealing movie because part two would just be the couple working out their relationship like the rest of us.

Marriages are crumbling at an alarming rate all over the country and the world. The breakdown of marriages is affecting millions of people in many ways. Not only does divorce affect us emotionally, but it also is the number one cause of financial ruin. And so, it is imperative that we do what we can to preserve our marriages and make them strong unions. What I have noticed is that rarely does a marriage fall apart because some outside force has attacked. Even in the case when one spouse leaves the other for another man or woman, that is usually the result of damage that has been done in the marriage months or years earlier. Just as it takes years for a marriage to grow strong and solid, it also takes time for a marriage to fall apart.

It is our job as spouses to protect our marriages and to make as many good choices as possible. We hear the minister say at a wedding that a husband is joined to his wife and the two are to become one flesh. What does this mean anyway? Although we should, in a perfect world, each be whole and healthy emotionally when we begin the adventure of marriage, in reality, each partner is like a box of parts. Your husband is a box of pieces and perhaps damaged parts that represent his past up until now, and you are a box of different, possibly broken pieces and parts. The job of each now is to take your box of parts and build something beautiful with the other partner. During the building process, making your different parts fit together is not an easy process, and it can be quite messy.

Many times in counseling sessions, one spouse will complain that he or she just doesn't love the other spouse anymore. I would like to suggest that love is not merely a feeling; it is not just a place we fall into; it is not just something we're in—it is something we *do*, regardless of how we feel. Feelings come and go. We can't base our marriages on feelings.

So, let's get ready to look at some of the dumb things we've all done and see what we can do to bring change. Let's strengthen our relationships so that not only are our homes happier places to be, but also we truly will be lights in a dark world.

dumb things he does #1

Not Being an Example for Your Family

(We're Watching What You Do!)

I live in the city of Los Angeles. In certain areas of my city there are thousands of homes where the mother is raising the children on her own. The dad took off for who knows where. The women in these situations are certainly doing the best they can, and some of them, on welfare, are managing to motivate their children, giving them a vision to get out of the ghetto. Kudos to these women! But the truth is, they shouldn't have to. The man should be in the home fulfilling his role, which I believe is to be an example, to protect, and in many instances to lead.

There are plenty of men around the world who are in absolute rebellion against this concept, and they are fleeing their responsibilities. I read an article about a famous actor who was quoted as saying that he was divorcing his wife and basically destroying his family because this particular time in his life was going to be "his time." He wanted to discover "who he was." There are times when we all want to abandon what's right and do something just for ourselves. Only the result of that self-centered action will be grief. This particular actor, on his journey to fulfill his needs, met another young lady and got her pregnant. Now he has another family to abandon.

As a man, if you are married, you need to be discovering who you are and what your strengths are from within the marriage. Strengths and weaknesses are revealed under pressure. Let the day-to-day work of your marriage reveal who you are.

Like a lot of women from my generation, I was raised with an attitude that anything a man can do, I can do better. Submission to a husband went out with the bra-burning ceremonies of the seventies! Well, needless to say, I was in for a bit of a shock after I got married. Because not only are men and women different, but also our roles in a marriage are different. And this goes all the way back to Adam and Eve.

Before Adam and Eve were banished from the Garden of Eden because they ate the Fruit they were not supposed to, Adam had plenty of leisure time. His toughest job was naming the animals. God provided his food and gave him all he needed, including a wife. After the Fruit and its consequences, Adam had to work the ground if he wanted to eat and provide for his family. No more goofing off! He was called to work, to provide for and lead a wife, who didn't really want to be led.

Part of the consequences in this story of Adam and Eve is that the woman desires her husband's position of leadership. As women, we are supposed to be adaptable to our husbands, even while inside we are battling with wanting the control, wanting their position. Because of this, I recognize that we are not always easy to lead; however, that doesn't change our role.

Likewise, in this story, the consequences for Adam were that he had to protect and provide for his family when probably he would much rather have been playing. For you, this means that your role is to set the example for your family—not go off and play with the boys, or even other women.

Leading your family is an active position. In fact, I believe that passivity is one of the top reasons marriages collapse. Don't ever let it settle in you. Be passionate about your wife and your home! Work hard at communicating with her so that the two of you stay connected. Don't adopt a "whatever will be" fatalistic attitude. Be brave enough to have a "whatever it takes" attitude. I have seen too many husbands destroy their families with their own passivity. They aren't watching who or what they let in their homes. Some of them are off pursuing some dream, and the wife is the only one bringing in the finances and managing the home. And let me tell you, when a man lets go of the leadership role, the woman will assume it, and it is not always the best for the family. The wife shouldn't have to do her job as well as yours.

I am aware that for decades we have confused you men until you didn't know what we, as women, really wanted. We hassled you until you became "soft and sensitive," which is what we thought we wanted. That desire of ours has been changing. I asked some women what quality in a man was the most attractive to them. Most of them answered with words like *confidence, passion, inner strength,* and *ability to make decisions.* Those qualities won hands down over *quiet, sensitive,* and *artistic*. Not that those aren't good traits to have. We just prefer those in smaller doses compared to the first ones mentioned. I apologize now for the confusion we caused.

In our home, as Philip and I were beginning to learn about equally important but different roles, things started to go a lot smoother. If you want your wife to be adaptable and flexible to you, you have to actually lead. Leading *isn't* controlling, being domineering, demanding, or bossing anyone around, however. You must lead by example. If you want your family to be supportive and cooperative, you must be the example. You must give more, love more, be more forgiving and more patient. It's not easy, but you can do it! If you are the coach of the family team, then it is up to you to encourage the strengths you see in your wife, not be intimidated by them. You are to encourage her strengths and look for ways for her to shine.

Gandhi, a great leader whose actions affected the world, led not by demanding or by being controlling but by serving. He led by example. He brought about global change because he first lived it. Lead your home by setting the example—by serving, not demanding.

Recently Philip and I started taking ballroom-dancing lessons. He took the initiative and signed us up for them. At the first lesson, I learned one of the most important rules. Our teacher told us that Philip's job was to lead, and mine was to follow. Imagine that! And even though Philip and I heard her give us the rule, it still took work to act it out. At some point in my growing-up years, I had learned some dance steps, so I picked up very quickly the dances our teacher was demonstrating. Philip had never done any dancing, so he had a harder time. The temptation for me was to lead because I knew what we were supposed to do, but our teacher soon stopped that. And she told Philip that in his leading of me, his movements and cues had to be definite, not hesitant. If he hesitated, I wouldn't know the right move to make, and we'd end up in a puddle on the floor!

Likewise, husband, I believe you need to be the example setter in your home. If you don't like the results you see in your family, quit blaming and change your actions.

**Set a good example in your home.
You can do it!**

dumb things he does #2

Not Knowing Your Job

(You Do Have One!)

Once you say, "I do," the real work of marriage begins. I know that you may be feeling exhausted from the amazing courtship job you did. You might feel that your job is done. *Not!* Regardless of the work you do outside the home (and we girls are truly grateful for you men who work and make money!), you have some very important jobs inside the home.

The number one need of most women is to feel loved. We function at our best when we are well and truly loved, and we feel that love. It is your job to demonstrate that love (and it *is* more than sex, although that is definitely a part of it!). Loving your wife means you are as concerned about her future as your own. Loving your wife means you *do* things that show it. Ask her what you can do that will help her feel loved. I can give you some ideas, but you are not married to me, so ask *her.* Actually just asking her what you can do is a way to show love. It shows you care enough to do something.

Sometimes Philip lets me sleep in (I love that!), and he gets the kids ready for and takes them to school. It may be a little thing, but I feel loved. He will talk to me for hours about my plans, hopes, and dreams—not his, *mine.* Another little thing, but I feel loved. He will say very nice things about me, in front of me, to other people. Little thing—I feel loved. And the truth is, he reaps the benefits of my feeling loved. When I feel loved, our sexual relationship is great! When I feel loved, I just want to give and give to him.

Loving means doing. Look for ways to demonstrate the love you feel. Don't keep it hidden in your heart. If there are times when you aren't feeling a whole lot of love in your heart, just the actions of doing loving things will bring the feelings back.

Plenty of men joke, saying, "Women—who can understand them?!" Well, you don't have to understand *women*—just one woman, the one you are building an amazing relationship with. It takes work, like all good endeavors that are worth anything, but you can do it!

Work on knowing your wife. What are her dreams, hopes, and fears? What excites her? What hurts her? What makes her cry? Know her.

Another way to know her is to understand that, as a woman, she thinks quite differently from the way you do. God did design her to be different from you because then, together, you and she complete the picture. Take the time to study the uniqueness of your wife. The more you understand her as a woman and as an individual, the less likely you are to be angry with her.

Remember, your wife is not you. She will do most things quite differently—but that doesn't make her wrong.

When a woman is feeling stressed or hurt by a situation, usually she wants your compassion and your understanding. She doesn't necessarily need you to fix it, so put the tool belt down!

One time, my feelings were really hurt by a friend's betrayal. I was devastated. As I sat next to Philip on the couch, he began to give me reasons why I shouldn't feel that way because this person hadn't been a good friend anyway. He said that she had been flaky and unfair to me, saying cruel things about me: Wasn't it good we weren't friends anymore? Now, while all that was true, did his comments help me deal with my hurt heart? No! What I needed was for him to hold me and let me talk about it. I needed him to say, "I'm sorry you're hurting. What happened was terrible." I needed an ear, someone to talk to, not a list of what I should feel and why. Nowadays when I'm hurt or stressed, Philip just holds me and listens and listens and listens. What a guy!

Women are different from men in so many ways. We talk a lot more than men do. (You've probably noticed this!) By the time you are home from work and winding down, your wife is just getting warmed up and has a lot more words to say! Although your wife should be your friend, she is not your "buddy." Communicate with her differently from the way you talk to your male pals.

One reason women talk is to create intimacy. So when you talk to your wife, going a little beyond the mere facts would be great! You might actually have to string together more words than "What's the score?" or "What's for dinner?" She wants to know your feelings. One of the by-products of intimacy is a wonderful sexual relationship, which I'm sure you're interested in. Please learn how to communicate your feelings. Ask questions of your wife about her day. Then listen, being patient when she's sharing.

These are just a few ways women are different from men. There are plenty of books out there that explain these differences in much more detail. Shock your wife; get one and continue learning!

Your wife probably has a different personality makeup from yours. She probably has strengths where you have weaknesses and weaknesses where you have strengths. Is she outgoing or quiet? Is she organized or spontaneous? What are her strengths? What are her weaknesses, and how can you help her? (It's not by preaching at her or getting angry at her weaknesses!) As you learn to live with and understand your wife, you will make the journey from being angry about the differences to understanding them to tolerating them to rejoicing in them!

Ask young couples whether there is anything about their spouses they would change, and most will respond with a loud *yes!* However, I have asked couples who have been married forty years or more what changes they would make in their spouses, and they can't think of one. What happened? I believe they learned to love the differences and be truly glad about them.

Understand your job as a husband, and even though it's a challenging one, go ahead—become great at it!

dumb things he does #3

Not Growing Up

(Okay . . . You Can Keep Your Sony PlayStation!)

You don't have to put away your X-Box, your surfboard, your rollerblades, or your skis, so relax! The growing up that I'm talking about involves thoughts, words, and actions that must change as we grow if we are to live in successful relationships. You can't be the eternal Peter Pan!

As you build your relationships, you must make the journey of growing from a boy to a man to a father. There is nothing wrong with each stage, as long as you are committed to moving to the next stage.

A boy is a child. He is entirely focused on getting his needs met. This is not bad; this is what children do. When our son was a baby, Philip and I had to meet all his needs. When he was hungry, we fed him. When his diaper was dirty, we changed it. When he hurt, we held him. We, as his parents, were responsible for seeing that his needs were met.

As he grew, he began to be able to meet his own needs. If he wanted something, he could get it. He wasn't concerned with helping other people get their needs met, but he could take care of his own basic needs and wants. This is not a bad stage to be in. There is nothing wrong with being a boy between the ages of four and thirteen. In fact, that is the only time a person should be a child.

Sometime in those early teen years, the boy should begin the transition to manhood. In many civilizations around the world, this transition is celebrated. In America, with the exception of the Jewish bar mitzvah, we don't honor this change. I believe we have a generation of males who are old enough to be men, and yet still act like boys, self-centered and self-indulgent, looking to have their own needs met. When those needs aren't met, they pout, throw tantrums, display uncontrollable anger, hit someone, and slam doors. This behavior is not acceptable in my child, and it is disgusting to see in a thirty-year-old male, yet I have seen it. I have seen males who should be men displaying all of the above-mentioned behaviors. And if that behavior doesn't accomplish the desired results, then they play all day, abandon responsibility, don't follow through, and aren't able to make a decision. Being a man means realizing the world does not revolve around you.

When our son was thirteen, Philip planned a celebration honoring the transition our son was making from boyhood to manhood. Philip and Jordan invited about twelve men, including Jordan's grandfathers, over to the house. These were men with whom Philip or Jordan had a friendship. Each man spent three to five minutes telling Jordan what he thought it took to be a man. These men made a covenant with him: if for some reason there came a time when he couldn't talk to his dad, their doors were open. Jordan also made a covenant with them to live his life in a way that honored God and his family. Philip then presented him with a ring to symbolize this covenant. It truly was a touching ceremony for everyone involved. After this celebration we worked hard at no longer seeing or treating Jordan as a child. We gave him more responsibilities, and the training for manhood began.

Most of you probably did not have a ceremony or celebration that marked your journey into manhood. In fact, perhaps you were never made aware of the importance of putting away childish things. But it is never too late to grow up! A boy is concerned with taking care of himself; a man not only takes care of himself but can do it while also taking care of others. A man is an entirely different person from a boy; he's not just a bigger boy. However, a lot of what we see in our culture are boys in men's bodies.

Because Philip and I live in a city where the entertainment

industry is prevalent, we come across a number of people involved in that industry. I worked as an actress for about fifteen years, and I love the creative, energetic, passionate aspect of that industry. It does, however, perpetuate the boyhood syndrome in some males. Some pursue their dreams at the expense of the real-life priorities. Whether you are pursuing your dream in the area of business, the entertainment industry, or even ministry, providing for your family must be a priority.

An actor I knew a number of years ago was married and had children. At one point in his career, he was making good money, and then he had a few lean years. He did not pursue other work, so his wife had to get a job to bring in finances. She began to be the sole breadwinner, supporting the family while he sat home frustrated about having no work. Because he was looking for ways to make himself feel better, he began to spend money on extravagances they could not afford. As the pattern continued, the marriage dissolved.

It is important to have a dream, a vision. If you don't, you will be frustrated, as well as frustrating to those around you. Yet the dream in your heart should never be at anyone else's expense. I have no problem with the idea of the man's wanting to be an actor, but when the work stopped coming in, it was his responsibility to find other work. As a man, your job is to take care of your needs and those of your family.

Perhaps there are many of you who did not have a strong man of integrity as a father to set an example for you. Don't let that be your excuse! There are men in your community who can mentor and support you. There is a men's organization in America called Promise Keepers. This group draws thousands of men together to work on issues of integrity. Plan to attend one of their meetings or perhaps find something similar in your community. Your family is depending on you.

The last transition a male can make is from being a man to being a father. A father is someone who gives to others without expecting anything in return. A father gives love when none is coming back. A father is more concerned about his wife's needs than his own. You can be a father whether or not you actually have children. The father is the man so secure in who he is that he can freely give. He's not worried about his own needs being met. A father is not just an older man, but a different person.

You have an amazing destiny to live out while you are here on the planet. You were not created just to take up space; you were created with a purpose. Your birth was not an accident—no matter what anyone has told you. As you discover the reason for which you have been created, a new strength will rise within you. You will be able to give freely to others. Remember, your purpose will always include helping other people and will never be at the expense of your family.

Not Growing Up

I heard a song by Randy Travis that asked the question, "When a tough choice needs to be made, will you make it with the spirit of a boy or the wisdom of a man?"

Discover where you are in your journey. Are you still a boy? (Perhaps be brave enough to ask your wife if she sees any areas of your life where you tend to act like a boy.) It's never too late to grow up. Get started. Drop the tendency toward self-centeredness. Find a wise man to whom you can be accountable, and get going! Are you a man making the transition to being a father? Don't give up! Be encouraged. You can do this. You were created to do this.

Your family and your world are counting on you to do your part. (No pressure there!) And, hey, if this seems too hard, begin the process by picking up your own dirty socks and look *really* hard for the mustard in the fridge before you call out: "Honey!!!" (Smile.)

So, grow up already! Make the journey from boyhood to manhood to fatherhood.

dumb things he does #4

Not Courting Your Wife

(Basically She Wants Romance 'til She Dies!)

We women have gotten hip to the fact that you men are conquerors. Most of you feel that after you have put all the time and effort required to capture us (marry us), you can kick back and relax. Often your passion for romance dwindles a bit. The problem with this is that *our* desire for romance and our need to feel cherished don't disappear after the honeymoon. The husband who switches from overdrive romance before the wedding to cruise control after marriage is asking for trouble.

The word *romance* has an interesting history. At the fall of the Roman Empire, Latin was the most widely used language in Western Europe. However, different places in Europe would come up with their own derivation of the Latin language. Eventually it became common knowledge that if you had a formal document—

whether it was a marriage license or a birth certificate—it would be written in Latin. But whenever things of passion were spoken, be it love, heroism, poetry, or chivalry, they would be told in the language of the common man, not Latin. They would be told in what was considered the romantic tongue. The romantic tongue speaks of what is passionate.

Men, when you get married, you will sign that formal marriage license. You will have the Latin document, if you will. But marriage is more than the formal; it is also romantic, coming out of your heart. And honestly a woman is driven nuts by having the legal, formal document and not having a man who can express his love and passion.

It is very important for a woman, your woman, to feel loved. In fact, feeling loved is her number one need. She is not wrong because she needs to feel loved. She is not wrong because she likes to be romanced. You might resent her need for love and affection, but it doesn't change the reality that she desires to be cherished. I suggest that rather than resenting this quality in her, you seek to fulfill the need to the best of your ability. In a marriage, you are the only one who can!

While the number one need of most women is to feel loved, your wife is probably different from me in how she needs to have love demonstrated to her by her husband. I will make a few suggestions for you, but check with her to see what she needs. Many times after I have read a book on men or marriage, I ask my husband if the information presented applies to him. I don't want to learn how to be a good wife to the men "out there"; I want to be a good wife to Philip.

There are some fairly easy ways to court and romance your wife, and there will be some ways that take a little more work. I love it when Philip brings me flowers for no apparent reason or leaves a note for me to find. But more than the flowers or the note, what touches my heart is that at some point in his busy day, he took time to stop and think of me. Birthdays and anniversaries are obvious times for romance, but the out-of-the-way times are really meaningful. I know that by bringing flowers or by leaving a note, he is saying, "I love you. You are important to me."

Sometimes in the middle of the day, I'll get a quick phone call from him to tell me he loves me. A soft touch, a gentle kiss, or a squeeze of the hand as we are both busy about our day really makes me feel loved. And, hey, I was really impressed when he bought a book of ways to be romantic. Little actions like these open my heart.

Most of us have learned over the years that men tend to be visual creatures and women tend to be auditory. This means that you are stimulated or moved primarily by what you see, which is why you like your wife to shop at Victoria's Secret, and why she is touched by the words you say. Most high school boys have figured this out. Unfortunately some have used this knowledge to manipulate young women into having sex. The boy says, "I love you. That's why I want to sleep with you." And the young girl, moved by what she hears, not by his physique or lack of one, complies. You can bet I will be teaching my daughter that she is not to believe everything she hears, and that her virginity is priceless.

One reason that women talk is to create intimacy and a sense of closeness. Because intimacy for your wife is linked to what you say, you would do well *not* to come home after a day at work and watch television, work on your car, or work on the computer all night. You might find that she will be a tad unresponsive in bed. If you want the reward of intimacy, you have to do the groundwork. You have to talk to her.

Romance is important to your wife, and rather than resent it, just accept it. The occasional gesture, such as a flower, phone call, date, gentle touch, or kind word, goes a long way toward creating a happy home. (By occasional, I mean daily!) Try something . . . anything. Be creative. Find out what she likes.

One husband whose wife had slowly been withdrawing from him over the past year came to ask about some ways to win her back. My husband challenged him to repeat some of his actions from their courting days. Philip then asked about broken promises.

Sure enough, there were some things the husband had promised to do but never came through with. Broken promises destroy marriages. One way to romance your wife is just to do what you say you are going to do.

A very smart husband called me and asked where his wife could get a professional makeup artist to do her makeup. She had mentioned to him earlier that she thought it would be lots of fun, and he knew she would be touched that he'd actually followed up on it. He was right; she was.

A few years ago, coming home from church after a Wednesday night service, Philip told me that he would be leaving for work early the following morning. When I woke up Thursday morning, he was indeed gone. I had begun preparing breakfast for our children and getting them ready for school when I noticed an envelope on the table with my name on it. I opened the envelope and read the note, which said,

> Dear Holly,
>
> If you love me, use the enclosed plane ticket and meet me at the top of the Empire State Building at 9:00 P.M. tonight. [Remember, we live in Los Angeles.]
>
> I love you.
>
> Philip

I read this note a few times and could hardly believe it! Philip, knowing my favorite movie is *Sleepless in Seattle* (a movie in which the young man and woman meet at the top of the Empire State Building), and knowing how much I love surprises, had certainly planned one for me. As soon as I stopped jumping up and down, I realized there was another envelope on my kitchen counter. I tore open that envelope and read note number two:

> Dear Holly,
>
> What are you doing standing there? [Now how did he know that?]
>
> You have four hours to get ready. I have arranged for someone to take you to the airport and someone to take care of the kids for the four days we are gone.
>
> We will have at least one fancy night so pack a nice dress!
>
> I have already left for New York, so that I will be there to meet you at the top of the Empire State Building.
>
> Love,
>
> Philip

After I read that note, I was laughing and crying at the same time. I felt so loved. He had planned such a wonderful surprise! Of course, I immediately called my good friends and asked to borrow nice dresses. (Women do this!) Seven o'clock in the morning is not too early for good friends! I got my kids off to school with extra hugs to last the weekend. I was taken to the airport and given a note I was supposed to open on the plane. (I actually waited and did this!) This third note was the sweetest yet. In it, he told me how much he loved me and how much he was looking forward to some days alone with me. He told me that he had some fun things planned and that we were going to have a great time. He also wrote that a limousine would be picking me up at the airport and taking me to the Empire State Building. On the plane, I proceeded to share my story with anyone around me who would listen, and by the end of the flight, there were more than a few people excited for me!

Once I arrived at New York's JFK airport, the driver met me and ushered me to the awaiting limousine. The music from the movie *Sleepless in Seattle* was playing in the limo. Philip had thought of everything. I was taken to the Empire State Building, and there I met the most wonderful husband in the world! We had four great days in an exciting city. He had planned things I like to do: high tea in a fancy hotel, a show on Broadway, a carriage ride through Central Park. He also planned some things he likes: a Yankees game and a visit to the *David Letterman Show*. All in all, we had a great time and left (together) more in love than ever.

Now, I understand that this example is a pretty elaborate way to romance your wife. You don't have to come up with something so fancy. In reality, it's the little everyday things that build and strengthen a marriage. Although I will admit, a big event every few years can only help! What touched me about the whole New York event was that he did simple things that made it special. Because he knew my favorite movie was *Sleepless in Seattle,* he planned our weekend accordingly. He could just as easily have said, "Holly, how about taking a trip to New York?" Then we would have taken an ordinary trip. What made it special was the surprise. (I love surprises!)

Your wife is the most important woman in your life; let her know it. I have had a few conversations with some men over the years who were having extramarital affairs. They were spending time, energy, and money trying to conquer the new woman. If each man had taken that time and that energy and courted his wife, he would have the marriage he wanted. Don't look outside your home for fulfillment.

I have also known women who weren't feeling loved (our number one need) by their husbands, and so when some smooth-talking men appeared, those women were seduced. Should the women have said no? Absolutely! But your job is to keep the walls of your marriage secure; don't leave the door open for trouble to get in. Find out what makes your wife feel loved, and then do it! Do what it takes to have a great marriage!

Here's a funny story that illustrates the unfortunate decline in romance. Make sure it's not you!

A husband's reactions to his wife's colds during seven years of marriage:

First year: "Sugar dumpling, I'm really worried about my girl. You've got a bad sniffle and there's no telling about these things with all the strep throat going around. I'm putting you in the hospital this afternoon for a general checkup and a good rest. I know the food's lousy, but I'll be bringing your meals in from Rozzini's. I've already got it all arranged with the floor superintendent."

Second year: "Listen, darling, I don't like the sound of that and I've called Doc Miller to rush over here. Now go to bed like a good girl, just for me."

Third year: "Maybe you better lie down, honey. Nothing like a little rest when you feel lousy. I'll bring you something. Have we got any canned soup?"

Fourth year: "Now look, dear, be sensible. After you've fed the kids and got the dishes done and the floor finished, you better lie down."

Fifth year: "Why don't you take a couple of aspirin?"

Sixth year: "I wish you'd just gargle or something instead of sitting around barking like a seal all evening."

Seventh year: "For Pete's sake stop sneezing! Are you trying to give me pneumonia?" (*Illustrations Unlimited,* Tyndale 1990)

And, husband, don't think you have to be the most handsome man on the planet. You don't. You just have to understand the power of romance! There are all sorts of incredible-looking men who have lost their wives to balding men with love handles who understand the importance of romance. Spend some of the same loving energy keeping your wife that you spent getting her! Romance her. You can do it!

Make a small gesture today to romance your wife, and plan a bigger one for the future.

dumb things he does #5

Living as If Work Is #1

(We Want You to Have a Job . . . We Just Like the #1 Position!)

We women love it when you men have a job. Really we do. We just don't want that job to become more important than we are. I have challenged (I hope in a nice way!) you about the importance of having a vision for your life, of providing protection and leadership for your family. These qualities are essential for your family. At the same time please don't let the work you do outside the home become more important than your marriage or your family.

Now I would imagine most of you would say, "Of course my marriage is more important to me than work." My question to you is, Are you *living* as if your family and home life are more important?

One man I knew was very successful at his work. He was asked to share his knowledge with people all over the world. And like most of us, he loved the affirmation he received from the people he worked with. Nothing is wrong with that. There was just one problem. At this time he was having challenges at home. Yet he was spending more and more time away from home because it was more fun to get the applause from the people he worked with than deal with the problems at home. So he traveled more and invested most of his time at his job. Being home was too hard and certainly no fun, so he rarely invested his time there.

In his defense, perhaps his wife was a complaining, nagging woman. And I understand that no man would choose to spend time with a bitter woman. (I talk to the women about this in their section.) However, I would like to suggest that abandoning the challenges that arise at home and using the excuse of work will eventually weaken the home until you no longer have one.

Sure enough, this man I mentioned is now divorced. From my perspective, and I'm aware that my perspective is an outside one, it looked as if he made work his number one priority. Even if the home front gets challenging—and it will from time to time—please don't allow yourself to put your relationship with your wife in any position other than the first one.

Years ago I talked to a newly married young couple. He was in school full-time and working a job part-time. She was also working. This is a common enough scenario. They came to talk to me because they were frustrated about their young marriage. I asked some questions, and then I heard him make a comment that was a signal like a huge red flag. He said that he had told his wife that for a few years his schooling needed to be the most important thing. He said that they needed to put the relationship on the back burner, just until he was out of school. I looked at him and said, "If you put your relationship as priority number two for a couple of years, you won't have one to come back to."

I gave them some simple ideas to keep the relationship a priority. I told him that I understood the demands on his time, and I challenged the wife to understand them too. I then told him that in the few hours he had each day with his wife to actually be *with* her. Sometimes we can be with someone in body, but not in heart and mind. I was encouraging him to actually be present in the moment. When he was in class, he should be there spirit, soul, and body—not wishing he could be somewhere else. And likewise, when he was with his wife, she needed him to be present spirit, soul, and body. He had to try not to be thinking about schoolwork in the few hours that were his wife's.

Yes, there are seasons in your work life that require a lot of your time. That's fine. It just can't be at the expense of your relationship with your wife. In the midst of a crazy workweek, *please* plan even a few hours just to be with your wife, focusing exclusively on her. Philip has always communicated to me and to our children how important we are. He will often shift work hours so that he can have time with me, or so that he can coach one of their basketball teams.

Sometimes I picture our hearts like a bank account. When men give love, romance, and time to women, the heart bank account is full. You want it to be full, because there will be times when you make mistakes or have to work lots of hours and so a withdrawal is made. The withdrawal isn't a big deal if the amount in the account is larger. So make sure you are regularly depositing love and time into the heart account of your wife. Because Philip has deposited so much time in our lives and hearts, when he might need to make a withdrawal of time—meaning when he might need to work extra hours one week—it's not a big deal; he has already spent a good amount of time with us, so he has time in the account to withdraw. I promise you that at the end of your life you are not going to wish you had made one more deal. You are going to be looking back over the relationships that were entrusted to you. I don't want you to have too many regrets.

This truth also applies to women. There are millions of women in the workforce today, and they are faced with the same challenge. It weakens our families when we put them in second place in our lives. Marriages and families cannot survive if left on the back burner too long!

Keep your marriage at the center of your heart and life. Invest whatever time is needed!

Why It's Great to Be a Guy

Okay, men, you've done a great job in reading this much. If you are feeling a bit overwhelmed right now, let me leave you with a few thoughts (which were anonymously sent over my e-mail):

1. Bathroom lines are 80 percent shorter.
2. When clicking through the channels, you don't have to stop on every shot of someone crying.
3. You can be showered and ready in ten minutes.
4. Your underwear costs $7.50 for a pack of three.
5. None of your coworkers have the power to make you cry.
6. You can quietly enjoy a car ride from the passenger seat.
7. Three pairs of shoes are more than enough.
8. You don't give a flip if someone doesn't notice your new haircut.
9. You can watch a game in silence for hours without your buddy thinking, *He must be mad at me.*
10. If you retain water, it's in a thermos.

Section 2

dumb things we both do

dumb things we do #1

Not Forgiving

(Go Ahead; Say, "I'm Sorry")

I'm sure it has taken you a while, but by now you have probably realized that your spouse isn't perfect. And if you are waiting for your spouse to one day be the perfect husband or the perfect wife, you are in for a very long wait. We are all going to make mistakes . . . some big, some little . . . as we live out our marriages. I have learned that marriages are built on forgiveness, not on perfection. We need to be quick to forgive each other. George Herbert said it like this:

> He who cannot forgive others breaks the bridge over which he must pass himself.

Forgiveness isn't just a nice thing to do. I believe it is a life-and-death issue. I remember talking with a man who had a life-threatening illness. This very ill man was extremely angry with someone who owed him three hundred dollars. It didn't appear he was going to get his money back, and he was furious, shaking his fists and going red in the face. When I suggested that he go ahead and forgive the debt and the debtor since it didn't look as if he was going to be paid back, he became even more angry. Should the debtor have paid his debts? Absolutely. Did the lender deserve to get his money back? Yes. Was it worth his life? I don't think so. I believe the bitterness inside him was killing him; he was literally eaten up on the inside with unforgiveness.

Forgiveness can be difficult for us because it pulls against our concept of justice. We want revenge for offenses suffered. (Oh, sometimes we won't admit it, but we do.) We want God to bless them with a lightning bolt! You may ask, "Why should I let them off the hook?" That's the problem: you're hooked. Or you may say, "You don't understand how much they hurt me!" But don't you see? They are still hurting you. You are still living the betrayal, the offense, whatever the crime. You don't forgive someone for his or her sake; you do it for *your* sake so that you can be free.

Forgiveness is pardoning someone. It is letting go of the resentment. Forgiveness is not necessarily forgetting. Forgetting may be the result of forgiveness, but it is never the means. Forgiveness is a choice, a decision of your will. Don't wait until you feel like forgiving to begin the process; you'll never get there. Feelings take time to heal after the choice to forgive has been made.

There have been times when Philip has hurt my feelings by something he has said or done or hasn't done. He was usually aware that my feelings were hurt. He would then say, "I'm sorry your feelings are hurt," not "I'm sorry that I hurt your feelings. I was wrong," which is, of course, what I wanted him to say. But I didn't want any seed of bitterness growing in me, so I chose to forgive.

I have also learned that I need to forgive, whether or not Philip says, "I'm sorry." (Men, now would be a good time to practice saying, "I'm sorry," out loud. Go ahead. For some reason it seems to be harder for you guys.) My forgiving Philip is not based on whether or not he apologizes. Of course, he should, and so should I. In fact, both of us have gotten so good at saying, "I'm sorry," we say it no matter whose fault it is. The movie *Love Story* popularized the statement "Love means never having to say you're sorry." Well, I think love means being the first to say you're sorry.

When we hold on to grudges, letting bitterness grow, we begin to withdraw from each other and withhold affection, which will ultimately destroy the relationship. Marriages are about forgiving . . . daily. If you find that, right now, you are feeling separated from your spouse, I would wager there is some unresolved offense between the two of you. Approach your spouse humbly and without blaming.

Describe how you are feeling rather than pointing your finger at him or her.

The ultimate betrayal in a marriage is adultery. If a spouse commits adultery, the spouse who was betrayed has a few choices. First, the person can choose to stay. Even though angry, the betrayed spouse ultimately chooses to forgive the betrayal, perhaps getting counseling and working on reconciling the relationship, and all the while, remaining committed to staying. Second, the betrayed spouse can leave.

Most people I have met who have been betrayed by adultery don't actually do either of those things. They might decide to stay, but instead of forgiving, they withhold affection and love. They do their best to make the spouse who committed adultery feel guilty by constantly using the sin against him or her. While there hasn't been an actual divorce, there has been an emotional one. The betrayed one is trying to punish the offender. They don't want to leave the marriage because that wouldn't be "right." Somehow in their mind, staying seems to be a better approach, even though they are angry, withhold love, and are bitter for years. I don't pretend to know the pain involved in this kind of betrayal. But I do know that whether the betrayed one stays or goes, he or she must forgive and get rid of bitterness so that the marriage has a chance of survival, or so that the next relationship isn't tainted with the scars of this one.

Years ago I read an article about a couple in marriage counseling. The wife was complaining to the counselor about her husband's "little black book." The counselor, thinking she knew what was in the black book, understood why the wife would be upset. The wife then went on to say that in this black book, her husband had written down every mistake she had made since the beginning of their marriage, and she just couldn't take it anymore.

When I read that, I became furious on the wife's behalf, wanting to go after that self-righteous husband. After I had finished muttering about the husband, I heard a small voice inside me quietly say, *You do that too*. I argued that I did no such thing, that I had not written down my husband's mistakes. And then I heard that voice say again, *No, you don't write them down on paper, but you are keeping a record of them in your heart*. I realized that was true. I had been keeping track of all the times Philip had offended me. I made the decision right then to never again keep a record of my husband's wrongdoings. No more keeping score. I was going to be so ready to forgive that I would begin forgiving even before the offense was finished (at least that's my goal—to be full of forgiveness).

As human beings, we need to feel forgiven. We have made plenty of mistakes in just about every relationship we've ever had. Walking around under the pressure of guilt is no fun. Here's a story that illustrates the great hunger for forgiveness we all have:

Not Forgiving

The story is told in Spain of a father and his teenage son who had a relationship that had become strained. So the son ran away from home. His father, however, began a search for his rebellious son. Finally, in Madrid, in a last desperate effort to find him, the father put an ad in the newspaper. The ad read: "Dear Paco, meet me in front of the newspaper office at noon. All is forgiven. I love you. Your father."

The next day at noon in front of the newspaper office 800 "Pacos" showed up. They were all seeking forgiveness and love from their fathers. (James Hewitt, *Illustrations Unlimited*)

Let's be people who freely give the forgiveness we all need. In the marriage relationship, each has specific roles to fill. Husband, your job is not an easy one—so, wife, give him a break. He is not going to get it right all the time. Forgive the failures. Cheer the attempts. And, husband, your wife, too, has a difficult job. There will be times when she blows it, when she isn't respectful or hasn't yielded. Please be quick to forgive, and encourage her to try again. Demonstrate forgiveness and love anyway. Each spouse will make mistakes. Give your spouse the forgiveness that you yourself will need—if not now, then the next time you blow it!

Forgiveness is not an easy task. My suggestion would be to first forgive yourself for your failures. Relationships are not always smooth sailing, and because we will make mistakes, not only do we need a spouse's forgiveness, we need our own. Recognize your weaknesses, work on them, and forgive yourself when you don't get it right the first or second or third time!

Be a great forgiver. The task is difficult, but not impossible. You can do it!

Be the first to say, "I'm sorry"; don't keep a record of offenses.

dumb things we do #2

Not Fighting Fair

(Yup, There Are Rules to Handling Conflict!)

"You started it!"

"No, you did!"

"No, you did when you changed your mind."

"Why do you always blame me?"

"I'm outta here!" *Slam!*

Sounds like a couple of children fighting, doesn't it? Actually I've heard words like these between adults. No matter how strong the marriage, conflicts will arise—from within and without. Learning how to deal with them is crucial.

I had a discussion one time with a woman who said she and her husband never argued; conflict never arose in their marriage. As I spent time with them, I noticed this was basically true. I also noticed a total lack of intimacy, honesty, and a superficial level of communication that would eventually lead to trouble or boredom. Resolving conflict not only opens lines of communication and relieves tension; it also can solve problems and air differences—all of which are important in strengthening a marriage.

Generally conflict within a marriage is caused by selfishness. "I want what I want and you want what you want," and when the competing desires collide, that's called conflict.

Most couples who use an electric blanket get one with dual controls because each person has a different idea of what the perfect temperature should be. We want what we want and don't understand why our spouses don't agree! With most of life, we can't get dual controls; we need to learn to resolve the conflict that occurs when our desires are different.

A great leader, Rick Warren, said he has noticed that there are a few different ways people respond to conflict. The first is "my way." This is the "I fight until I win" response: "I have to be the winner. You are totally wrong, and I will fight you until you cry 'uncle'!"

The next response to conflict is "no way." People who respond this way always avoid conflict. There is no way you are getting them into a fight. They withdraw, pull back, and ignore the problem. Doing this may keep the marriage calm, but nothing is ever resolved.

Another response to conflict is "your way." People who respond this way always give in. They are doormats. They want approval so badly that they roll over and play dead. Again, doing this may keep the relationship calm, but it also produces a lot of bitterness and will probably lead to an eventual out-of-control explosion.

"Halfway" is another response. "You give in half the time, and I give in half the time." This is certainly a better response than previous ones, but there is a better way to communicate.

"Our way" is the best way to handle conflict. This is when we work out mutual goals together. We do what's best for the marriage, not just for one of us. "We" is more important than "me." The more couples who actually get this concept, the more who will not let a conflict separate them, realize that no one issue is more important than the marriage as a whole. Some marriages break down because of the conflict that might arise due to the pressures of one spouse's job. Maybe the wife is offered a huge promotion if she moves to the office across country. Rather than just taking the job, perhaps both spouses need to decide what would be better for the marriage. Perhaps the move would benefit the family, but maybe it would only benefit the wife. So this is where the couple needs to come back to their agreement that "we" is more important than "me." This is not always easy . . . but it is necessary if a marriage is going to last.

To resolve any issue, we need a sit-down-and-face-the-issue conference. And usually more than one. Conflict is rarely solved accidentally. It must be deliberate and intentional. Conflict is rarely solved on the run. Be prepared to fix the problem, not cast blame. Come ready to reconcile and resolve.

Certain ground rules have to be observed in conflict resolution. The United States and Russia have had treaties to ban certain weapons in the event of conflict, and it's not because both countries were in total agreement on certain issues. They just realized that nuclear weapons could destroy both. Perhaps it is the same in a marriage. We must eliminate verbal weapons that will do more harm than good. Watch for using words such as *always* and *never* because usually they aren't true. And then of course, remember what you tell your children: no hitting, no biting, no lying, no throwing things, no using bad words!

In an argument, oftentimes one or both of you are angry. Anger isn't the problem; it's what happens when you're angry that can be problematic. Do you yell, hit, or call each other names? That's abuse, and that's a problem. Do you let your anger push you toward resolving the conflict, or do you attack with it? It is important to learn to manage your anger in resolving conflicts, or you will have bigger problems on your hands.

In any conflict, stay focused on the issue being brought up. Don't bring out a list of all the things your spouse has done over the years. Unrelated issues are off-limits. Don't blame or accuse. It's better to make the discussion about your personal feelings than it is to point a finger. Use statements such as, "When ___ happens, I feel ___." Or "I need ___." Or "What would make me feel better is ___."

Using phrases that begin with "You should" or "You need to" or "You always" will only escalate the conflict. Try to remain calm and logical. (I am aware that this is not always easy, but it is part of the price of being a grown-up.) You'll get better results if you can express yourself honestly and directly.

Pick your arguments carefully. Don't fight over every little thing! Don't make every issue of your lives *sooo* important. That becomes exhausting and minimizes the issues that are really significant to you. Perhaps each of you could pick three or four things that are the most important. Maybe for one of you it could be having a family night, not being late, and no whining. For the other it could be having a home-cooked meal three times a week, having a date night, and sticking to the budget. Whatever the three are—both of you must agree to uphold them. Anything else that comes up (and stuff will!) should be negotiated. Remember, you are on the same team.

Don't start resolving a conflict late at night when you're both tired and emotions are frazzled. Strive to resolve the issue when you both are at your best emotionally and physically. Unless anger has escalated to rage and you are incapable of managing yourself, don't leave the room. Commit to continue until the conflict has been resolved, peace is restored, or you have agreed to work it out at another time. It is childish to walk out, slamming doors. Adults resolve issues, seeking peace.

Because most of us aren't that great at effectively resolving issues without causing hurt, I would suggest praying before beginning a discussion that you think could turn into an argument. Pray that the words you use will not be careless or hurtful, and that you both will find peace.

As a general rule, don't argue in front of your children unless you are willing to make up in front of them. Our children need to see how we resolve conflicts, not just how we start them. However, I would set very narrow limits on what the children see or hear. I knew a couple whose child watched them fight—not resolve conflicts, but fight. The child heard them yelling and calling each other names. If you haven't learned how to resolve conflicts in a calm way, don't fight in front of anyone, and please get help from a counselor. Children are helped when they see mature people resolve a conflict. They are destroyed when they witness the two people they love the most, who should be providing security, yelling and attacking each other.

There are also conflicts that arise because of pervasive attitudes evident in our culture. These conflicts arise from outside the marriage. I actually believe that the pressure on our marriages is much more severe than it was for our parents. The media aren't helping.

How many happy two-parent families do you see portrayed on television?

Humanism—the desire to put me first—is a prevalent theme in our society today. We can't be foolish and think that it won't affect us. Many marriages are abandoned because one or both spouses have succumbed to the humanistic thought pattern of, "I will do whatever is good for me, regardless of what my desires do to the marriage." This is the "if it feels good, do it" mentality. And while this selfish attitude might be acceptable to a certain degree in a single person, it will destroy a marriage. *We* always has to be more important than *me* if a marriage is going to weather the storms of life.

Materialism—the quest for more and more stuff—is another external pressure that can destroy a marriage. We become so focused on working hard so that we can gather things that we end up not having time for each other anymore. The media in a subtle way convince us that the more stuff we have, the happier we'll be. In our culture, money is seen as *the* answer to everything. Rick Warren, in one of his seminars, told of an ad for a fur coat he had seen in a newspaper:

> The divorce is final coat . . . your marriage blew it . . . fine. Satisfy yourself and go buy a fur coat! OK so it didn't work out. The important thing to remember is there are a lot of other people out there who have gone through

> the very same thing. Shed the tears and slip into a fur. An Antonivich fur. Any one will do, they're all so extravagant. The fox will do nicely. So you lost the man of your dreams. Find the fur of your dreams at Antonivich.

Materialism says, "Relationships don't matter . . . what matters is possessions." That kind of materialism destroys marriages. J. Paul Getty was the wealthiest man in the world during his lifetime. He said, "I would give my entire fortune for one happy marriage."

Both humanism and materialism are prevalent in our society, and so we need to be prepared and ready to keep our marriages from being affected.

Other conflicts can attack a marriage. These are the crises that can come upon most of us at one time or another. The day will come when we will likely face a crisis we didn't anticipate. We don't like to think about the possibility of having our lives disturbed by such unpleasant circumstances. Here is a list of the various crises that families face, according to Norman and Ann Bales in an article they wrote called "Coping with Unexpected Crises":

death of a child
a disabling accident
loss of employment
a house fire

major illness
natural disaster
spouse being sent off to war
loss of income

When these things occur, the marriage relationship will change. It can never be the same again. The crisis will either make the marriage stronger or cause it to fall apart. The hope is that because we are going to learn how to handle conflict and crises, our marriages will be stronger!

Here are some steps to handling the crises that Norman and Ann Bales mentioned in their article:

Talk openly about the crisis. Oftentimes one partner will want to avoid talking about the problem. Just as with conflict occurring within the marriage, avoidance is an invitation to disaster. Couples need to talk about the extent of the damage, what they can realistically control, and make plans for handling those things they are able to manage.

Avoid the temptation to place blame. Don't point fingers. We also need to protect each other from self-blame.

In spite of the pain, keep some fun in your life. The problem is serious, but keeping a sense of humor takes the edge off. After the devastation of the 1994 earthquake in Los Angeles that caused severe damage in our home, I remember Philip looking at the piles of shattered china and commenting, "Well, you said you wanted new dishes. Now I believe you!" We laughed for a moment and then began the long process of cleaning up. And we didn't stay at the cleanup process all day either. We took our kids, drove to a hotel in another county (one where the earth wasn't moving!), and got in the Jacuzzi. We took a few moments, amid the work, to make some fun. It helped.

Stay in touch with those who need and love you the most. Sometimes in the middle of a crisis we are tempted to isolate ourselves. *Don't!* We were not created to go through life alone. Both spouses need friends to help them through the tough times. I got a doctor's report one time that scared me. Thank God, I had a friend who was willing to listen to me vent my frustration. She listened to my feelings and generally helped me find my way out of the darkness. You need your friends. Your friends need you. Don't abandon them in their dark times either. You could be their lifeline.

Don't "medicate" yourself with drugs and/or alcohol. A doctor might prescribe some medication that could be helpful in getting through the crisis, but that is perhaps only the temporary solution. Ultimately we need to let ourselves deal with the crisis.

Handling conflicts—those from within and without—is a skill that takes practice and humility. With internal conflict, be willing to take the time needed, be willing to be wrong, and be willing to pray for peace and wisdom. You can do it! And with external conflicts and crises, be wise. Don't let your marriage fall victim to the attitudes in society that can kill it. Use the skills I've talked about when a crisis might come your way. Don't be caught off guard.

In a calm manner, focus on the issue at hand, staying committed to resolving the conflict. Use wisdom, and protect your home from the attack of society.

dumb things we do #3

Expecting Great Sex to Just Happen

(Don't Always Believe What You See in the Movies!)

I'm not sure where you got your information on sexual relations between married couples. Maybe you got some of your information from all those wonderfully romantic movies, and now you are realizing that they lied! Rather than the perfectly choreographed movement between two people who know exactly what they are doing, your experience with sex has been more along the lines of, "Ouch . . . honey, your elbow is on my hair," and "Move over . . . I'm falling off the bed!" And did you notice how in the movies sex is never messy? How come in the movies no one ever needs a towel? What's with that? So, maybe we can conclude that the movies are not the best places to get sex education.

Perhaps you were one of the very few people on the planet raised by incredibly functional parents, who not only loved you but also loved each other emotionally and physically. They readily explained everything you needed to know about sex and answered all questions openly, lovingly, and without shame. And perhaps you and your spouse were virgins when you got married and thus entered the marriage with no past baggage or hang-ups. If all this is true, perhaps on your honeymoon sex was perfect because you were so well prepared and knew exactly how to please each other. Now if this is you, you can certainly skip to the next chapter, or you can read this with an idea that you can possibly help others.

However, if you laughed with astonishment that I could even think there are people who had those kinds of parents, because you think those people don't exist (and maybe you wondered whether your parents ever had sex!); or if you got your sex education from your friends, who were *sooo* well educated; or if you indeed had a past when you entered into marriage, then this chapter is for you. You are like most of us, and you know what? There is hope!

I do want to say that I am very aware that there are people, perhaps many of you, who have suffered abuse in the sexual area. It makes me angry on your behalf that something designed to be wonderful between a husband and a wife is perhaps reminiscent of pain for you or causes serious obstacles you need to overcome. I am sorry. My encouragement to you is to please get help. There are many avenues from which you can get that help—wise counselors, good books, and churches with programs that can lead you to freedom. Don't stay bound another day. Life is too precious for that!

I've read my share of romance books and definitely seen most of the "chick flicks" out there. And the truth is, as enjoyable as they may be, most of them present an inaccurate picture of sex. The sexual part of marriage is wonderful (duh!). However, the wonderful part comes with just a little bit of knowledge, a willingness to be humble and learn, and a desire to please your spouse. And honestly it takes practice. (That's the fun part!)

Although sex isn't the only part of a marriage, it is an important one. There are three reasons for sex. *One reason is to produce children.* God commanded Adam and Eve to be fruitful, multiply, and replenish the earth. (That's the only command humans have had no trouble keeping!) So, yes, sex can and often does result in children, and we want that—but the sad thing for too many couples is that the main purpose for sex is this one. They have kids to prove that they have been sexually active, but there is no unity, harmony, or pleasure involved. Instead there are anger, hurt, frustration, and misunderstanding.

Another reason for sex is to promote unity in a relationship. Many times in wedding ceremonies we hear the verse, "For this reason a man shall leave his father and mother and be joined . . . adhere . . . cling . . . cleave . . . to his wife, and the two shall become one flesh."

I have found that to create unity in a marriage, the secret to cleaving is leaving. If you enter a marriage and still leave other options open—mental, emotional, or physical options—it will be tough to make your marriage work. You must leave all other options and cleave to each other. No other friendship should have more influence over you than your spouse.

Philip was not the first boyfriend I had ever had, and when we got married, I didn't understand this concept of leaving my past in order to create unity in my marriage. Perhaps I understood the theory of it, but certainly not how to live it out. In the early years of our marriage, whenever Philip and I got into a disagreement, there were times when I thought back over a relationship with an old boyfriend. In my head I would make comments like, *If I had married* him, he *wouldn't hurt my feelings like this. Maybe I should have been with* him. Thoughts like those are goofy because the truth is, if I had wanted to marry the other guy, I would have. And everyone gets his or her feelings hurt at least a few times in a marriage.

To truly create unity in a marriage, not only must you leave all other options behind—whether they are emotional, mental, or physical—you also must leave your parents. I have seen many marriages in trouble because the wife runs home to Mommy or Daddy whenever she is having trouble in her marriage. While I understand getting wisdom from your parents if they have had a successful marriage, you must communicate to your spouse that he or she is the most important family you have and that his or her opinion matters the most.

I heard of a husband who was calling his mother and having long conversations with her almost daily (she was not sick or incapacitated in any way; she was just having a hard time letting her "little boy" go). You do need to honor the position your parents hold in your life, but once you are married, they should no longer hold a place of preeminence. That place belongs to your spouse. The wife of the mother-calling husband could certainly feel disconnected from her husband because perhaps by the time her husband talked to her, he was exhausted emotionally from the conversations he had had with his mother.

The only person's emotional needs you should be meeting (other than your children's) are your spouse's. Don't get exhausted trying to meet anyone else's. To create a unified marriage, you must leave the past and cling, adhere to your spouse.

Sex is a unifying bond between husband and wife. It solidifies the union. When the rest of the world might seem crazy, it is wonderful to feel connected with your spouse. Perhaps you have had a really tough day at work, your boss yelled at you, someone cut you off in traffic and pointed a finger at you (and I'm not talking about the index finger!), and you had a flat tire. However, if you can come home and later that evening have sex with your spouse, your world can perhaps be righted again because someone is on your side. A purpose of sex is to produce unity between the husband and the wife, which is why premarital sex can really mess you up because you become bedmates before you become soul mates.

Oftentimes, after a funeral or disaster, many couples make love because the experience reaffirms *their* life and union. It's as if to say, "We are okay; we are together; we are alive." This sense of union can perhaps give us the will and strength to face whatever challenge may be ahead.

The third reason sex was created was to provide enjoyment! Sex should be pleasurable! This is perhaps where many couples miss out. Often people may have the idea that married sex is boring. How wrong they are! I would like to offer some practical ways we can make it even more enjoyable. One way is to create the right atmosphere. Sometimes men underestimate the importance of atmosphere because atmosphere often means nothing to a man. It could be anywhere. Most women, on the other hand, are very conscious of the atmosphere: Is the door locked? Is the light too bright or too dark? Is it too hot or too cold? Are the kids running around? We need to be willing to set the right atmosphere that makes our spouses eager for love. Rick Warren, who is the pastor of Saddleback Community Church, said he did an extensive study (!) on how to make a woman eager for love.

To create the right atmosphere and make that woman of yours eager for love—men, pay attention—here's all you have to do: caress, praise, pamper, relish, savor, massage, make plans, empathize, serenade, compliment, support, tantalize, humor, purr, hug, cuddle, excite, pacify, stroke, protect, phone, correspond, anticipate, nuzzle, smooch, Jiffy Lube, forgive, sacrifice for, entertain, charm, show equality for, trust, grovel, brag about, help, acknowledge, polish, embrace, upgrade, accept, butter up, hear, understand, beg, bleed, nourish, resuscitate, respect, kill for, dream of, promise, deliver, tease, flirt, commit, snuggle, snooze, elevate, enervate, serve, love, bite, taste, nibble, gratify, take her places, swing, slip-slide, slather, squeeze, moisturize, lather, tingle, slicken, gelatinize, indulge, wow!, dazzle, amaze, idolize, and then go back, Jack, and do it all again!

That's how you make a woman ready for love, which might seem overwhelming especially when you realize that to get a man eager for love, all you have to do is show up naked (smile)! I am presenting this in a playful manner, but the truth is, you are probably different from your spouse in what creates a romantic atmosphere, so be willing to adjust. And remember, great sex starts hours before intercourse. A loving touch, an "I love you" phone call, a note, or a soft kiss goes a long way in creating the atmosphere both want.

Atmosphere is only one important aspect in enjoying sex. It is also important to understand that because men and women are different, our sexual needs are too. Generally men are stimulated visually, and women are stimulated by what we hear. Now, this doesn't mean that women are blind and that men are deaf. I'm talking about primarily. If this isn't true for you, then talk about your major stimulus. Because men are visual creatures, they like us to go to bed in something other than that Laura Ashley flannel gown we got when we went away to college. It's not that you can't ever wear that thing—just not very often! Splurge on some new lingerie, really! Find out what he thinks looks good and get some. (Throw out that underwear you have had for five years!) I have some pieces of lingerie that are certainly not my favorite, but I am not wearing them for me! *He* likes them, so on they go. (And the truth is, they aren't on that long anyway.) And you know what, you feel sexier when you are in pretty lingerie.

If you are not content with the shape of your body, then do something about it. Change your eating style . . . begin an exercise program . . . whatever . . . so that you will be happy about your body. If you continue to find that you don't really want your husband to see you, if you are more comfortable wearing a tent, then make changes. You can do it, and your relationship is worth it.

Men, since most of you do like sexy lingerie, this means you are actually going to have to step foot into a lingerie store. Go with your wife and show her what you think looks good. And, girl, you be brave enough to wear it! After all, he is the only one who will see you, and if he thinks you look great, then it's settled! Now, I am not saying that every time you make love you need to put on sexy lingerie, but you do need to put more effort into it on a regular basis.

Men, because we are not blind and we do see you, it would be helpful if you threw out those old boxers and came to us clean and smelling good. My challenge to you, however, is to get really good at verbally communicating your love to your wife. You might be turned on by what you see. Well, we like it when our husbands tell us intimate things rather than just getting down to the business of sex.

Try looking at your wife and telling her she is beautiful. Let your eyes caress her even before you ever touch her. Tell her how she is making you feel. Tell her she is sexy. Tell her you love her body. Just tell her! *This is not the time, however, to point out those fifteen pounds she needs to lose!* She is very aware of the flaws of her body. To help make sex great for her, speak lovingly and passionately to her. Generally a woman's greatest and most important sex organ is her mind, so stimulate that (and I don't mean by quoting Einstein!). Be intimate with her. Share how you really feel.

John Gray, in his book *Men Are from Mars, Women Are from Venus,* gives a man a few ideas of what to say in the bedroom if you really want to get your wife in that loving mood:

"You are so beautiful."
"You are my dream come true."
"I love you so much."
"I love sharing my life with you."
"You turn me on so much."
"I love touching your soft skin."
"I love holding you in my arms."
"I love your legs."
"Your breasts are perfect."
"You feel so good."
"I love having sex with you."

Gray says that he always gets "lots of applause from women when he recounts this list of things to say. Men don't realize that women love and need to hear such things again and again. Men might be thinking some of the things on the list, but women need to hear it."

So, men, my suggestion is to get good at communicating your feelings and thoughts through words. Perhaps you could use some of the suggestions listed, or you can come up with your own.

Whatever. As you communicate verbally, your wife will love it, and your sexual relations will definitely be more exciting!

Great sex isn't always as easy as one, two, three. Men, what worked last night—that caress, then a touch here, then a loving word—may not work tonight. And that's what makes it interesting! Sex is more than a formula. It is an intimate expression of the feelings in your heart.

Be responsive to each other. There was a time in history when the mothers of young English women told them to "think of mother England" while they were "enduring" sex. That probably was not very exciting for their husbands! Girl, your husband will love it when you are responsive to his attempts at loving you. Don't just lie there. Respond to him verbally and physically. Tell him what feels good. Don't be shy. There is perhaps no greater turn-on for a man than a responsive woman. He wants and needs to know that he excites you. If you are not the one who usually initiates intimacy, go ahead and shock him. Be the aggressive one! When you are on a date with him, whisper in his ear, "Honey, guess what I have on under this dress? Nothing." Or put sexy underwear in his briefcase. Undress him as soon as he comes home. Try something new—anything. Expressing your interest in sex is a great stimulus for him. Be playful!

I plan on being married to Philip for a very long time, and so I will be the only woman he makes love to. Although he is an amazing man with great integrity, I never want him to be even tempted to stray from me. I know I am not responsible for his actions, but I also know there are things I can do to keep our sex life wonderful.

Kevin Leman, in *Making Sense of the Men in Your Life,* put it like this: "Wife, in the twenty-first century, sexual disinterest on your part is flat out dangerous. Maybe in the Garden of Eden, where sexual images didn't abound, sexual apathy could be managed. But this isn't the Garden of Eden, and your husband isn't living in a pure world. *If you want him to be faithful, the least you can do is never give him a reason to look elsewhere.*"

Most of us women would probably be shocked at how important sex is to our husbands. (On the other hand, maybe you wouldn't be!) Do your part in keeping it from becoming routine, and keep him satisfied at home.

Each of you men, equally important to your wife's attempting to be sexy and playful for you is your verbally romancing her. Don't let her be tempted by some suave Don Juan she might work with. No woman will leave a man who is effectively communicating love and passion to her. In your times in bed, communicate to her that you find her very sexy and that she is indeed the most important part of your life.

I recently heard a phrase in a song by Faith Hill and her husband, Tim McGraw, that said something about making love all night long. Now, doesn't that sound like fun? But realistically, how often has that happened?

Here's a thought. I like to see times of sexual intimacy in three ways: the banquet, the dinner, and the snack. There are times when we can have a *banquet* of lovemaking. You know, those times when the kids are at someone else's house or when you're in a hotel, the music is playing, and the candles are lit, and you can leisurely enjoy each other—maybe even more than once—because no one has to get up early. But like real banquets, those times are special yet don't occur very often. Then there are times we can have *dinner.* We take time with each other, but it's not an all-night-long occurrence. And then there are the *snacks.* Don't underestimate how wonderful a snack can be! This is the traditional "quickie." Sometimes all you have is minutes before both of you have to get back to whatever you were doing. Take advantage of those minutes. Keep your sex life varied by enjoying banquets, dinners, and snacks—all are important. We certainly couldn't live by snacks alone, and having a banquet every night is unrealistic, so keep it interesting!

We also need to realize that each of us goes through seasons in life, and so our sex life will too. Since one of the goals of sex in marriage is to communicate love to each other, we need to keep that at the forefront of everything we do. When we are first married, before children come along, generally we can focus exclusively on each other. Once the wife is pregnant, things could change for a bit. Sex might be uncomfortable for her in the latter months. Or maybe not—husband, don't assume—you should ask. After the baby is born, it will probably be a few weeks before intercourse is a possibility. Make sure to express your love in other ways. Be creative. And, wife, don't make the mistake a lot of mothers do and put your husband on the back burner. Your husband needs to know he is the most important person on the planet to you. Yes, you might have a new baby and are juggling that wonderful new person, but you still need to be conscious of that man you married!

I made the mistake of putting Philip on that back burner for about six months after our son was born. We had sex, but I just wasn't very engaged; I was too conscious of the baby. It took a while to get the intimacy back once I became conscious of what I had done. Don't do this! When our daughter was born, I was much more savvy to this tendency, and our relationship stayed strong and intimate because of it. I made sure to make time for Philip, both emotionally and physically.

There are also times when one of you might be stressed with

work, and so the sex drive might be minimal. Don't put pressure on the other. Be understanding. Maybe one or the other of you is unusually tired. Philip and I made an agreement way back in the first year of our marriage that we would never say no to the other (unless there were unusual circumstances). And basically we have kept that agreement because both of us realize that *we* are the only way to get each other's physical needs met. But we don't try to force the issue or make the other feel guilty by just not being in the mood. Be flexible with each other. And keep in mind that in most situations too much time should not pass before you are sexually intimate again. Every couple's "too much time" will be different. Don't compare yourself with others. You and your spouse work it out between the two of you.

Some couples—both the husband and the wife—use sex as a weapon. One or the other will withhold sex because of something the other did. Now, I can understand it might take just a little bit of time to recover after a disagreement, but don't let too much time go by before you are physically intimate again. Don't punish each other by holding back physically. Physical intimacy between husband and wife is a wonderful unifying bond and should never be used as a way to manipulate or control.

Our actions with each other should demonstrate cherishing. Although it is okay to be creative (in fact I definitely encourage creativity in the bedroom), it is *not* okay to do anything that would demean the other. Over the years, some people have asked me my opinion as to what is okay and what isn't okay in the marriage bed. I would not presume to legislate your actions, but I can give you my opinion. Because I am trying to protect this part of my marriage and keep it wonderful, I draw certain lines. I think the marriage bed is for husband and wife only. Bringing another person into it, even in the form of fantasy or pornography, corrupts what should be honoring to each other. Remember that the goal of lovemaking is to demonstrate your love for each other, so whatever actions you take in bed should be respectful of each other. If one of you is not comfortable with something, then it shouldn't happen.

I also protect this part of my marriage by *not* talking to my girlfriends about it. (I do talk to them about most everything else!) The marriage bed truly is no one else's business. If there are challenges that need to be worked on, and most of us have them from time to time, then find a safe person to talk those over with. (A "safe person" is someone your spouse feels comfortable with as your chosen sounding board.)

Great sex doesn't just happen, but when you understand each other, it will be wonderful. So lay your egos at the door, listen to each other, and get to work! (This is the fun part!)

Enjoy this part of your relationship! Realize that, like the other aspects of marriage, it, too, will get better and better over time!

dumb things we do #4

Not Understanding Our Differences

(Vive la Différence!)

We are each uniquely created with different abilities and different personalities. We have different strengths and weaknesses that need to be dealt with along this journey called life. We need to become good at knowing, understanding, and loving the differences rather than wasting time trying to change each other or wishing each other was different. Carl Rogers said it like this:

> When I walk on the beach to watch the sunset, I do not call out, "A little more orange over to the right please," or, "Would you mind giving us less purple in the back?" No, I enjoy the always-different sunsets as they are. We do well to do the same with people we love. (cited in *Illustrations Unlimited*)

Understanding the differences in our personalities helps us function more effectively as a team. Husband, your wife is not you. She won't think or act like you on most occasions. Wife, your husband is not you. He won't respond the same way you would most of the time.

Organizations all over the country are administering personality profiles to their employees so that employers can better place people in jobs where they will flourish, and the employees will function better together. A personality profile is simply an indicator of basic tendencies. It is also helpful to understand the different personality types so that whether we are married or just part of a relationship, we can begin to understand each other. There are many different types of profiles, although they are all basically similar. Hippocrates, hundreds of years ago, developed a system that is helpful and easy to understand. He said there are basically four major personality types.

Every person probably has one dominant personality type and a secondary one, so the combinations are multiplied. No one is put into a box. There is no right or wrong personality. No personality is better than another, and each has strengths and weaknesses. Remember, we are learning this to understand how to more effectively love our spouses and others in our lives.

The first personality type I'll talk about is the *sanguine*. These people are usually the easiest to recognize when walking into a room, because everything about them is moving: their arms, their hands, and their mouths. These people are excited, energetic, spontaneous, and fun-loving. These are the party-waiting-to-happen, confetti-throwing people, and they can prevent many dull moments. If you don't know any of these, you should hire some for your next party. They will keep it from getting boring. They communicate with lots of !!!!!!! and **BOLD CAPITALS!** They are outgoing and love to be with people. They can get any project started with a bang. On the other hand, they are not great at finishing those projects. They can forget obligations and can be undisciplined. They often speak without thinking. (Their motto is "Ready . . . fire . . . aim!") Emotionally they need a lot of attention, affection, and approval.

Another personality type is the *melancholy.* These people are analytical, and they like things done perfectly. (They invented whiteout and spell-check.) They are schedule-oriented and organized. Their checkbooks can be works of art, everything written in the column for which it was intended. There is very little clutter on the top of their desks. They tend to be talented and creative, often genius-prone. Their clothes are enduring (rather than trendy) and precise, and have few (if any) wrinkles. (Linen can drive them nuts!) They can also be hard to please, negative, and depressed over imperfections. They expect perfection, and since life is rarely perfect, this can send them on a downward spiral. Emotionally they need sensitivity, support, and silence.

Quite often these two marry each other. (We did.) It definitely makes for a lot of excitement! Not too many dull moments—we actually pray for just a few dull ones. I'm the sanguine, and Philip is the melancholy. It doesn't get much more different than that. The great thing is, where I am weak, he is strong, and vice versa. However, initially it drove me nuts. He likes all his "ducks in a row," and I wasn't even aware there were ducks! I kept trying to make him wrong, thinking that he should have been more like me. (Anyone see a problem with this?)

Our closet was an interesting place to work out our differences. His clothes were arranged very neatly. Shirts with short sleeves in one section, then shirts with long sleeves in another, then dark-colored trousers, light ones, then jeans, and then suits were in their own section. And of course, the ties were placed on one spinning rack, and belts on another. Shoes were neatly arranged on shelves. (I had no idea what those shelves were for.) It was an amazing masterpiece!

My style of closet management came closer to the if-when-I-kicked-my-shoe-off-it-hit-the-doorframe-I-called-it-put-away style. I'm sure that those of you who are melancholies are cringing and shaking your heads at the thought of what I did. My husband did too. Gradually (and I must confess, it was a gradual process) I realized that his organizational skills were a definite strength. He could actually find his clothes in his closet! (Me—I hunted through piles for the least wrinkled one, not that I would actually iron it or anything! Now you melancholies are really feeling sorry for my husband, aren't you?) So eventually, rather than continue to call him picky, I let his strength influence my weakness. Now my closet, though it will never be quite as together as his, is vastly more organized. (Most of the clothes are hung up.) One time, in order to surprise my husband, I installed racks for my shoes. When he came home, he was as excited as a melancholy could get. You'd have thought I'd given him a thousand dollars!

He has learned to value my outgoing nature. We meet more people and have more friends because I am such a people person. He likes being with me because I make things more fun. I'm going to let *him* say a few words here, just so I won't be doing *all* the talking about myself:

My wife is an amazing person. I have a lot of respect for her and I appreciate her gifts, personality, and unique abilities. (How am I doing so far, honey?) It did, however, take some adjusting (you know, "work") for us to discover how the two of us could be a team and have a great relationship.

Holly is outgoing and energetic; she loves people; she's playful and likes to have fun. What a great person to be around! Right? Well, I love people and I like to have fun too—but we just go at it in two very different ways.

Do you realize how annoying it can be when someone always wakes up happy and ready to play? Especially when it takes others a little more time to get in the flow? Some people (and I won't mention any names) can be outspoken and energetic when the social situation at the moment might call for a little sensitivity or timing.

As for me, sometimes I can plan, strategize, and think for too long when some passionate, immediate action is needed. While I can be more project-oriented, her focus on people has helped me include more people in my life and put more effort in building friendships. I like to have a good time, but sometimes I can be thinking through "the important things" I need to take care of—and then her playfulness reminds me to have fun on our journey. And her outgoing style encourages me to step out there and make things happen when I could get stuck just being pensive and analytical.

I remember once during a marriage seminar, we were having a bit of a question-and-answer time. It was a great session and we were having a lot of fun. One person asked us something like, "What's one thing that has annoyed you about the other that you have had to work through?" Holly gave her answer with great discretion and insight, and then it was my turn. I thought for a few seconds and then, not really sure what I was going to say, I slowly began, "Well . . . I guess . . . it would probably be . . . " and

Holly interjected, "When I finish his sentences!" Well, there you go. The place fell out with laughter. It was acted out right in front of everybody.

We do make a great team because we've learned to work together instead of acting like we are on opposing teams. We have learned to bring our strengths to the relationship with some sensitivity instead of fighting for our way.

The third personality type is the *choleric*. These people walk with purpose and focus, never forgetting why they were going from point A to point B. If they were headed from the bedroom to the laundry room with an armload of dirty clothes, they would actually make it to the washing machine. (The sanguine would start out with the laundry but stop to pick up something off the floor . . . then the phone would ring . . . then lunch would sound good . . . then a friend would come over . . . and about three hours later he or she would see the pile of dirty clothes and remark, "Oh, yeah, I was going to do that laundry this morning!") Cholerics are born leaders; the rest of us have to learn how to be one. They exude confidence and excel in emergencies. They can see the whole picture and assume leadership where there is none. They can also be bossy and impatient, finishing your sentences for you. They will tell you what needs doing instead of asking for your opinion. They have a hard time relaxing; they can be workaholics and may find it difficult to say, "I'm sorry." They also might run over people on the way to reach a goal because, after all, the goal is the most important thing. Emotionally they need loyalty, appreciation, and a sense of control.

The fourth personality type is the *phlegmatic*. These people are the least obvious to identify. They are not extremely anything. They tend to be chameleonlike, capable of adapting in many circumstances. Their clothing is the most relaxed that is acceptable. They are easygoing, sympathetic, good listeners, and they make great friends. They are the peacemakers. They can also be unenthusiastic, indecisive, lazy, and resistant to change. (It might take a stick of dynamite to move them to something new.) Emotionally they need peace and quiet and a lack of stress.

If these two marry each other, they will also have challenges. One wants to be on the go, conquering new goals, and the other wants to quietly do it how it has always been done. The choleric has to be careful not to run over the phlegmatic, but rather learn to appreciate the quiet strength that's offered. And the phlegmatic can learn to try something new and go to new places.

Whether you have married someone who is very similar to you with a lot of the same strengths and weaknesses (scary thought) or someone quite different, it takes work to go from hating any differences to understanding them to valuing them. Learn to treasure how your spouse was created.

Don't expect your spouse to be like you. I don't expect Philip to be Mr. Social. I know that after he has been at a function a few hours, he's ready for some quiet time. I don't resent that about him; I just accept it. And at the same time, he doesn't resent my need for affection; he has learned to be good at giving it.

Don't hold on to your weaknesses, saying, "Well, that's just how I'm made!" We need to recognize weaknesses and overcome them all along the way. We need each other to get the job done.

Discover your unique personality and that of your spouse, and begin working together to form a stronger union. I am a better person because I have let myself be influenced by the strengths of my husband. And he knows his life is richer because of what I have brought to it. This attitude may not be born overnight, but it can be born! You are each stronger because of the other; know that.

Not only do we generally deal with personality differences, but you and your spouse probably come from different backgrounds. This also makes for an exciting journey of two becoming one. Two parents who still love each other to this day raised me. Rarely did I hear them argue. Daily I was told that I could be whatever I wanted to be when I grew up. No limitations, as far as my future was concerned, were put on me. Because of my dad's job I was raised in countries all over the world, so my view of life was a big one. My parents were financially secure; I never lacked for anything, and I was encouraged to go to the best university I could.

Philip, on the other hand, had parents who fought loudly. In fact, the police would come to tell his parents to chill out. Eventually they divorced, and Philip lived with his mom. Rarely did anyone help him with his homework, and he was not encouraged to further his education. He did not see a loving marriage in action. Until we were married, he had never traveled outside the United States. The lack of money was often a challenge in their home. When I look at the difference in our backgrounds, I realize that *I* honestly have no excuse for failure! I was raised with every advantage. Philip's background *could* have limited him, and I have the utmost respect for him because he has risen above every limitation placed on him. He continues to raise the ceiling in his life. He truly is my hero. So the two of us, with these very different backgrounds, married. It certainly wasn't easy.

I had never really seen a husband and a wife resolve conflict, and Philip had seen his parents fight loudly and out of control. Neither of us knew how to fight fair. We had work to do. He had never seen his dad show affection to his mother, and I had seen plenty of love expressed, so while I was comfortable with it, he wasn't. We had work to do. Because I was raised with money, I liked to spend it. Because Philip wasn't, he liked to save it. We had work to do. We each had different ideas on parenting. We had work to do.

We began to realize that in building our own home, we should take the best from the homes of our past and use those good parts.

Philip liked the emphasis my parents placed on education, so we have decided to make education important in our home. I liked Philip's idea of living within a budget (well, actually I didn't like it; I just saw the benefits!), so we have incorporated that concept in our home. There is good and bad in each spouse's past. Take the good and build on it. Remember, you are building a new home, not your parents' home.

Sometimes I look at just how different Philip and I are, and I am amazed that we are not only making this marriage work, but we love being married. Perhaps the reason is that rather than focusing exclusively on where we are different, we look for the similarities and rejoice in them. While we love the differences, we truly find joy in where we have melded. We love God. We love each other. We love sex! We love our children. We love going to their sporting events. We are committed to our friends. We are committed to helping people become champions in life. We love our church. We love to travel. We love to read. We love basketball. We like going to the movies. We like the color purple. So, my encouragement to you is to realize that you and your spouse are probably different in many ways—gender certainly, and perhaps personality and background. That is okay. In fact, those differences make your unit stronger. And my encouragement to you is to also make a list of similarities and rejoice in them!

Treasure the differences in each other, and let them bring strength to the relationship.

dumb things we do #5

Expecting a Great Marriage to Just Happen

(Cinderella Is a Fairy Tale!)

I loved Philip. He loved me. Then we said, "I do." I thought that was all it took to have a great marriage: love and a wedding ring. Boy, was I in for a shock after the first month! We all expect our physicians to have gone through years of school and residency in order to be good at what they do, and yet most of us expect to have a strong marriage without ever learning how. Wouldn't it be great if all universities required the students to take a Marriage 101 class? In the long run, that class would certainly prove more useful than the calculus class I took. But for those of us who missed the Marriage 101 class, there is hope.

One of the most important things to do in a marriage is to continue learning how to be a better spouse. (I tell singles that the number one question to ask yourself about a potential spouse is, *Is that person a learner?* A person who is a learner will learn to be a great wife or a great husband . . . a great parent . . . a great employee at a job . . . whatever.) Each of us must continue to grow in the role of husband or wife because it is one we will have for a lifetime.

When looking through a microscope, scientists can tell a living organism from an inanimate one by observing any change. After a time if there is no growth or change, the object is considered a dead one. It is the same with you and me as individuals and as part of a marriage.

We must grow, both as individuals and as a part of a couple. As individuals, we must be willing to learn new things and think new thoughts. By thinking old thoughts, we won't make it through life the way we are supposed to. We need to meet new people, read new books, take new challenges, and set new goals. In other words, we need to be lifelong students.

A few years ago an article in *Parade* magazine told the story of a group of nuns who consistently lived to be more than one hundred years of age. Scientists went to their convent to study them and see what was different about how they lived. The scientists got permission to perform autopsies on the nuns who died. During the autopsies, they discovered something interesting. The brains of the nuns had many more connections between different points than most people's brains. These specific connections formed when the brain was learning something new. The scientists then discovered, after speaking to some of the nuns, that this group of nuns was continually learning new things, right up until death. They were learning to speak new languages, work new machines, and read new books all the way into their nineties.

Because their brains were continually growing and being used, the nuns lived longer. You and I need to be people who want to learn new things, not just so that our lives will be longer, but so that they will be fuller. The growth that I make and the changes I embrace won't change who I am, but they will make me a better me.

As part of a marriage, we need to grow in a couple of ways. We need to be students of our spouses, not only in learning their personality strengths and weaknesses, but also in learning their likes, dislikes, and needs. We need to learn about them, not to change them, but to know them, from the simple to the more complex—from knowing their favorite food to knowing what they need when they're hurting. Does he like some space to figure out a problem? Does she need you to listen to and hold her? Does he like surprises? Does she like everything planned out? What are your husband's dreams? What are your wife's fears? What is she looking forward to? What is he hoping for? The tricky part about this is, you have to be willing and prepared for your spouse to grow and change—just as you are doing. Even the favorite cereal might change!

As part of a couple, we need to continually learn about building relationships. Many great books, tapes, and videos out there are designed to strengthen you as a couple. I have shelves and shelves of them. I figure that being a wife is one role I will have for the rest of my life, and I want to continually improve.

Oftentimes people will come to me for some help in their marriage. I am always amazed when I find out that neither spouse has read a book or listened to a tape on relationships. If they wanted to know how to build a car, they would study and read books on how to do it. Yet most people want to build a great marriage and aren't taking advantage of the wonderful products available. There are conferences, seminars, and retreats available for you to attend. They will provide not only great information, but also a boost that all relationships will enjoy. Please read books, listen to tapes, or go to a seminar. Expending this effort will definitely be beneficial.

Another way to build a great marriage is to spend time with a couple who have been happily married longer than you have. I qualified that statement with "happily" because spending time with people who are down on marriage or negative about a spouse will not be helpful, to say the least. Just as first-time mothers learn from experienced mothers, so we can learn from couples who have been married longer. Find some couples you can spend time with. Extend yourself. You will love the results.

Also, first-time mothers need to spend time with other first-time mothers, so that together they can encourage each other through all the new experiences that come with a baby. I cannot overemphasize how important it is for us to spend time with couples who are at the same place as we are on the journey of life. There is no replacement for friends who will see you through the obstacles and rejoice with you over the victories. One of the first questions I ask a couple coming to me for coaching is, "Who are you spending time with?" Most of the time I find that the couple is not spending much time with other married couples. And perhaps because women tend to be more naturally relational, the wife could set up dinner or an outing with another couple. So, wife, make that call. If you find that you don't know many other couples who share your values, then go places where you might meet them. Stretch yourself. Your marriage is worth it! Your marriage will grow and be strengthened as you build relationships with other like-minded couples. Go for it!

Be committed to growing more as a person and as part of a marriage. Growth and change produce life.

Section 3

dumb things she does

Published in Nashville, Tennessee, by Thomas Nelson, Inc.

Library of Congress Cataloging-in-Publication Data

Wagner, Holly.
Dumb things he does, dumb things she does, and just a few dumb things we both do! / Holly Wagner.
p. cm.
ISBN 0-7852-6520-1
1. Marriage. 2. Communication in marriage. 3. Couples. 4. Man-woman relationships. I. Title.
HQ734 .W182 2002
306.81—dc21 2002001357

Printed in Mexico

02 03 04 05 06 QWM 6 5 4 3 2 1

Dedication

This book is dedicated to my readers;
to those of you committed to building
strong marriages in a society
that so desperately needs
to see you succeed.
You can do it!

dumb things she does

Contents

Section 3: Dumb Things She Does

Author's Note

My husband, Philip, and I have been married seventeen years—most of them happy ones. In these years we have made plenty of mistakes; you'll read some of them. Together we pastor The Oasis, a great church in Los Angeles, California. Because pastoring has been our job since we were married, a lot of what I have learned (the good and the bad) about marriage has come as we have worked at the church.

Preface

Remind me that divorce is expensive and murder is against the law!" was a plea I made to a good friend a few years ago. I laugh about that comment now, but back then I wasn't kidding. Not only did it seem that our marriage just wasn't fun anymore, but maintaining it was too much work. Perhaps there have been times when you, too, have felt like that. Perhaps you are feeling like that now! Well, take heart; you are not alone, and there are some answers.

In this book I will present some clear, simple suggestions that certainly helped my marriage and that I believe will help yours. This book is not the ultimate guide to wedded bliss; it does not present all the answers to every problem. This book is just a small piece of the puzzle. There are many books on marriage out there; read some. There are wonderful seminars and conferences available

to help us married people; go to one—or more. A great marriage doesn't happen just because you want it; you have to want it enough to learn and grow.

I split this book into three sections: "Dumb Things He Does," "Dumb Things We Both Do," and "Dumb Things She Does." Read whatever section applies to your situation, or read them all. (It's not that big a book!) And after reading, talk. Talk to your spouse about what you've read. Do you agree with this point or that point? Have you done this particular dumb thing? (Let your spouse answer as to whether you have done one of the dumb things!) Remember, marriages are worked out over a lifetime, so relax. Even you—no matter how many dumb things you've done—can strengthen your marriage!

dumb things she #1 does

Not Liking Yourself

(What's Not to Like?!)

It is not your husband's job to give you a life. It is not his job to make you feel good about yourself. While he wants to be your hero, it is not his job to fix you. We have all heard that we are supposed to "love our neighbor as we love ourselves." This means that I won't be effective at loving anyone else if I don't love myself—if I don't love who I was created to be. Philip is not responsible for my self-esteem. I am.

When you like who you are, you are more fun to be around. You laugh at mistakes, not taking yourself and everything around you so seriously. You're comfortable with yourself. One evening a few years ago, Philip was speaking at a seminar in our city. I was there with him to be supportive and to talk to the audience about his books and tapes that they could buy to further their education. I was addressing the audience and explaining what was on some of

his tapes. It was my first time to do that, and after describing a few tapes, I decided to give some away. I then thought that rather than handing the tape to someone, I would throw it to her. Obviously I need to work on my throwing arm. Instead of the tape reaching the woman I had intended it for, the tape beaned some poor, unsuspecting man on the head.

I felt terrible! My first time on the job, and I blew it! The poor man, with his eye watering, was trying to be brave as I handed him a tissue, cracked a few jokes on myself, and carried on. (I think my husband slid under his chair at that point!) Now, did I make a mistake? Yes. Have I since learned some cassette-tape distribution etiquette? Yes. Did it rob me of my confidence? No. When you make mistakes and goof up, be willing to laugh. I'm not talking about serious, life-threatening mistakes. Those aren't funny. But sometimes our inability to laugh at ourselves is a sure sign that we lack confidence or self-esteem. We need to learn to like who we are, warts and all.

There are a lot of reasons for low self-esteem. Past abuse, neglect, rejection, and abandonment are just a few confidence stealers. All of us at one point or another have experienced some of these; some of us have experienced devastating abuse. Nevertheless, the important thing is to begin a plan to build self-esteem. The self-esteem I'm talking about is not the self-centered, as-long-as-I'm-happy-it's-okay mentality, nor is it arrogance. I'm talking about the

quiet confidence you get from knowing your identity, knowing you are on the planet for a purpose. There are certainly men who need to understand this, but in my limited experience, I have seen more women struggle with the issue of self-esteem.

According to the 2001 edition of *The New York Times Almanac,* more than five billion of us on the planet believe in God. I would like to ask you to take that belief one step farther and not only believe in God, but also believe that He created you and that He did it for a purpose. You are not an accident. (No matter what your parents told you!) You were put on the planet at this time in history for a specific reason. You have a destiny, a purpose to fulfill. We won't know our purpose, our destiny, if we don't know our Creator.

If I want to know specifics about my car, I don't ask another car. I ask the company that made the car. When I read the manual, I'll know how it works and what all the buttons are for. (Not that I'll be able to do more than put gas in it, but in theory I'll know more!)

I would like to suggest that the first step toward liking yourself is knowing that you were created for a purpose, and that it is a good one. Then I would encourage you to discover what that purpose is by getting to know your Creator. You and I were put on this earth for amazing reasons. We have so much to contribute, so much to share, no matter what our age. We are amazing women, and it is not about doing; it is about *being.*

One reason we must know who we are is to determine what we'll do. We can't do this backward. I can't rely on what I do to determine who I am, because if what I do is snatched away or if I fail at it, then I'll see myself as a loser. Tiger Woods is a phenomenal golfer, but what happens when he can no longer golf? He will struggle if his only identity is in being a golfer. What about the Michael Jordans, Julia Robertses, and beauty queens of the world? What happens when they can no longer do what they now do? Will they lose personal confidence? Will they be confused or depressed? What about you? Is your identity wrapped up in what you do?

We don't get our identity from a driver's license; most of the stuff on that is embellished anyway! (Be honest. How much does yours say you weigh?) We don't get our identity from a passport; that just tells us where we've been. We don't get our identity from school report cards; most of us are still dealing with the negative things some teachers said. We don't get our identity from a mirror; we just use that to put on makeup. You and I get our identity from our Creator. Through our Creator's eyes, we get a true picture of the individuals we are.

Each of us is

- not a victim, but a conqueror—in fact, more than a conqueror.

- not a loser, but a winner.
- not an addict, but an overcomer.
- not a captive, but set free.
- not a sinner, but forgiven.
- not a random creation or her parents' "accident," but put on the earth "for such a time as this."

You can't get self-esteem from reading books, although they're often helpful. You can't get it from going to seminars, although you'll learn a lot. I believe that self-esteem comes, first of all, from living in the identity your Creator has given you, regardless of the circumstances. Second, according to Dr. Laura Schlessinger in her book *Ten Stupid Things Women Do to Mess Up Their Lives,* self-esteem comes from daring to have a dream, following through on reaching that dream, and suffering through all the sacrifice and pain necessary. Then, when you finally reach the goal, the dream, you are so impressed with yourself that your self-esteem and your self-confidence rise.

One of the weaknesses I noticed about myself was that I didn't always finish the projects I started. I am a great starter. It's just my finishing that needs work! Because I saw myself as weak in this area, it affected my self-confidence. I knew I needed a plan. I

knew I needed to start something and then actually finish it. And it needed to be something significant—you know, something other than finishing a double-scoop cone. At that time in my life, I was taking my son, Jordan, to karate class. As I watched the classes, I began to think, *I can do this*. Plus, I noticed that at every level a student passed, a new color of belt was given, all the way to the black belt. It was like a prize, and I like prizes.

So, I signed up for karate. Perhaps that wasn't the easiest of goals for me to reach, but that was what I did. I started as a white belt, and at every class I attended, I looked at the black belt on the wall and said, "You're mine!" The first day of class I showed up in my new white uniform and stiff white belt. I was so excited because I had seen the movie *Karate Kid* and I wanted to learn to do the amazing kick that was demonstrated at the end of the movie. I just knew it wouldn't be long before I wowed my family and friends with my amazing ability. Well, we didn't learn that amazing kick the first day or even the fortieth day. What a bummer! For months we learned how to fall. That was not what I signed up for. I spent hours learning how to fall to the front, how to fall on my back, and how to fall to the side. Fall . . . get up . . . fall . . . get up . . . fall . . . get up . . . *boring!* I definitely wanted to quit. That had been my pattern for years.

As soon as a project got a little mundane or slightly boring I

would quit, feeling justified (because why should I have to put up with boring?), and look for something more exciting. Here's a little tip for free: sometimes life, marriage, and work are boring or just become routine. Since we are grown-ups, the decisions we make during those times actually say a lot about our character. Previously the decisions I made during the boring part of projects revealed that I was a quitter. I was determined to change that! So, there I was again, at a boring part of a goal. But I hung in there. I didn't quit. I kept the goal of the black belt in front of me.

And months later I discovered the reason for the fall/get up process as we began to spar. In my first sparring match it wasn't long before I was foot swept (that's a nice way of saying knocked on my rear end!), but because I was so used to falling and getting up, I got right back up. No matter how many times I got knocked down, I got right back up. Just like those punching toys with sand on the bottom that your kids have played with. There had been a purpose for the boring part. Hang in there; don't quit; there is probably a reason for the boring part of the journey you are on. And take heart . . . it doesn't stay boring forever!

A few years into the karate challenge, my son decided that he wanted to devote most of his time to basketball, so he no longer wanted to study karate. Great, now my karate goal became an inconvenience. It wasn't easy to figure out what to do with the rest

of the family while I continued to take classes. I almost quit at that point. Another tip for free: reaching goals is never convenient.

Three years into the challenge karate began to get physically difficult. The actual moves I was required to learn were tough. The forms (a series of intricate movements) I had to memorize were so complicated, I was wondering if it wasn't too hard a goal for me. And I ended up with more bruises than I wanted. Karate is a contact sport, and that was becoming more and more evident.

Four years later, I passed my black-belt test. Yippee!!! Were there times when it had been boring? Yes! Were there times I wanted to quit? Yes! Were there times it was inconvenient? Yes! Were there times when it seemed too difficult? Yes! Just the fact that it *was* a difficult goal to finish made it even more valuable to me. Getting my black belt did things for my self-esteem that nothing else had done up to that point. I had started something and finished it.

You can too. Pick something, anything. Find a goal, and begin the process of reaching it, overcoming all the obstacles on the way—boredom, inconvenience, difficulty, and others. When you finally get there, you will feel amazing!

When a woman is confident in her purpose and has a healthy self-esteem, there is no occasion for envy. Think about it. Why are we envious of others? Usually because we want what they have, and we aren't truly enjoying who we are. I am always amazed at

people who can really sing. I mean, there are women who can actually stay on key for an entire song. It baffles my mind! Because I can't sing a note (or at least not the right note), I could be envious of a woman who can sing, wanting what she has. But I would be wasting my valuable time, wanting a talent or ability someone else has, instead of being thankful for the abilities I have.

No two of us were created with the exact same purposes, personalities, or destinies. Each of us is unique. Each of us needs to spend time discovering who she is and what her purpose is, instead of trying to be like someone else and wanting her gifts. That only leads to frustration and envy. Come on, girls. Let's rejoice when one of us accomplishes something, is honored for a talent she has, or gets married. Don't be envious and wonder why it didn't happen to you. I believe you have been specially created to fulfill a unique purpose. Find out what it is.

A certain proverb asks the question, "Who can find a virtuous woman?" *Virtuous,* in this context, doesn't mean "quiet, weak, or able to crochet," which is what I always thought (which is also why being virtuous seemed boring to me). Virtuous means, "a force on the earth consisting of three things: people, means and resource." She is this person of might and valor when she first of all understands that she must build a strong people-base in her life. In order to take the incredible place on the earth we were designed to, we must surround

ourselves with amazing people . . . people committed to growing and learning. We are a part of an awesome army!

We are also women of means. This means we know how to make money and spend it. (Personally I have been really good at the second part of that! . . . just gotta work on the making it part!!) And the third aspect of virtuous involves resource. This means that as virtuous women, we are learners. We resource our body, soul, and spirit. We are strengthening our body by healthy living. Our minds are enlarging as we read books, go to seminars, and learn from women who have the climbed the mountain we want to scale. We spend time getting to know the God who created and loves us. We are not sitting around idly watching life go by . . . we are LIVING it! So, she is a force on the earth . . . a warrior woman!

I am not to wait for a man, my husband, to make me virtuous. No, that responsibility is in my lap. Marriage should be a place where two wholes meet, not a place to get neediness met.

Make a plan to build your confidence in who you are. You can do it!

dumb things she #2 does

Not Demonstrating Respect to Him

(R-E-S-P-E-C-T, Just as the Song Says!)

According to Mr. Webster, *respect* means "to show consideration or esteem for." We all should be respected. Respecting each other is part of giving each other the sense of dignity that we all deserve. As you demonstrate respect to others, you will find more and more people will open their hearts and lives to you. So, respect is crucial in building healthy relationships. However, I have found in talking with many couples that respect is one of the first things to go.

Generally the wife loses respect for her husband or neglects to demonstrate it, and I would like to suggest that your husband's number one need is to feel respected. He becomes the man he was created to be as he feels that he is respected. Of course, there are things he needs to do to earn your respect (I'll talk to him in the other section!), but the thing is, you need to demonstrate respect to

your husband, whether he "deserves" it or not. If there are occasions when you are having a hard time respecting what he does, then respect his position as husband in your home. I don't always respect the decisions the president of our country makes, but I always respect the position of the presidency. Likewise, generally our number one need as women is to feel loved, and our husbands are to demonstrate love to us at all times, even when we are unlovable. (Yes, it's hard to believe, but sometimes we are hard to love.)

Both spouses have a tough job. I know there are times when I am not very lovable, but that doesn't change what my husband is asked to do. And there are times when it takes a conscious decision of my will to demonstrate respect to my husband, even though what I want to do is to very loudly give him several pieces of my mind! Nevertheless, my job, because I am committed to building a strong marriage, is to demonstrate respect to my husband.

Let me tell you a story I heard . . .

The mayor of a large city and his wife attended a banquet at a hotel. In order to avoid the rush of people after it was over, they left the back way and walked to his office. On the way, they passed a building under construction. One of the construction workers yelled out a greeting to the wife. She waved and continued walking with her husband. The mayor asked his wife who that man was. She replied that he had been her boyfriend at one time. Feeling

rather proud, the mayor asked his wife, "Aren't you glad you married me? Because if you had married him, you would've been the wife of a construction worker." The mayor's wife replied, "No, the truth is, if I had married him, he would be mayor."

This story illustrates the point that behind every successful man, there is a woman. I also believe that behind almost every failure of a man, there is a woman. When a man feels respected, he can accomplish so much. As women, we have an ability to be a great influence in the lives of our husbands. What an awesome position that is!

If you want your husband to be all he can be, you need to be an encouragement. When you talk about your husband, make sure you speak in an edifying way. It is very hard for me to be around a woman who is constantly whining and complaining about her husband. My husband has weaknesses. I'm not blind to them or denying them, but I'm not calling my girlfriends and griping either. I'm doing my best to speak uplifting words about him because I want him to rise to his potential, and I know I have a part to play in that. How are you talking about your husband to your friends and coworkers?

You demonstrate respect not only by how you talk *about* him, but also by how you talk *to* him. A certain proverb says, "She opens her mouth with wisdom, and on her tongue is the law of kindness." *Kindness* literally means "loyalty." The words we use should show

loyalty to our husbands. When you're loyal to someone, you demonstrate that you're on the same team. A surefire way for me to start a fight with Philip is for me to come into a conversation attacking with both guns blazing. (I always carry at least one.) This proverb is asking us to approach our husbands as if we are on the same team. Philip is not my enemy. (No matter how many times it has felt that way.) He and I should be on the same team, fighting a common enemy—not each other.

Look at your heart: Do you secretly feel that you are on the opposite team from your husband? Begin to change that. Do you secretly (or perhaps not so secretly!) roll your eyes at some of the decisions he makes? That is a pretty demeaning method of communicating. Demonstrate respect by working together to overcome a problem. Demonstrate respect by being loyal.

How you talk to him is important. A woman I know came to me for advice about an explosive situation with her husband. In the middle of some marital difficulties, she told her husband she had decided to spend a few days alone to get herself together. She did not want to answer the phone or to be with anyone, including friends. Not surprisingly the husband, who felt as if she was demanding something (she was), got angry and resentful. I applauded the woman's desire to spend time working on herself. But I smacked her (not really) for how she handled her desire. She did not demonstrate

respect to her husband, but instead demanded something from him. And he pulled away.

I suggested that she go back to her husband, apologize for the way she spoke to him, and ask for what she needed in a respectful, honoring way. I encouraged her to say something like this: "Honey, I am so sorry for being demanding. I know that wasn't respectful. Please forgive me. [This is called eating humble pie and is often necessary.] I am really feeling overwhelmed right now and know that I am not able to give you all I should. What would you think if I were to take a couple of days to rest so that I can get my strength back?"

She must have said something like this because her husband's response totally changed. When she went to him as if they were members of the same team—both wanting the best for each other—he responded with love and support. He even offered to get her a hotel room and take any phone messages for her while she was away. He offered to support her in any way necessary. When we are respectful, showing loyalty and demonstrating honor, great things happen.

The key here in showing respect is *asking* about an issue rather than *telling* what you are going to do or *demanding* that something be done. One of the turning points for my friend was that she asked her husband, "What do you think if I take a couple of days?" She asked him for his input. That opened the door to his heart.

Just as you have ideas or suggestions for your husband that you believe would help him at his job, I do too. Many times as we are leaving our place of work, the church, I will have an opinion that something I noticed in the church should have been handled differently. I have learned to approach this most delicately. I used to just blast forth with my opinion, assuming my husband wanted to hear it. But when I did that, an invisible wall went up, and he didn't hear a thing I said. I realized I needed to do something different if I wanted my husband to hear and receive what I believe was God-given inspiration. The next time I had an opinion about the way something should go in church, I asked Philip if I could share it with him instead of demanding that he listen.

Now, in spite of my weaknesses, my husband does know that I am his soul mate, and he does want to hear what I have to say. When I asked, he said yes, and then I shared whatever nugget of truth I needed to. He was grateful, and then we talked about the situation. There have been times, however, when I have asked if he wanted to know what I thought and he said, "No, not now. We'll talk later." I was okay with that. We need to give our husbands the freedom to say no, and not get resentful about it. Because my husband has seen the results of my comments and realizes that my comments aren't necessarily just opinions, but valuable insights, he now asks for my thoughts and input regularly. I don't force

them on him; I respect his position enough to ask. So did a great woman of history, Queen Esther, and because she treated her husband with respect, she saved a nation.

Esther became queen basically because she won a beauty pageant. But she proved to have far more than her beauty going for her. Soon after she was made queen, she found out that her husband's right-hand man, Haman, had devised a plot to kill all the Jews. Esther, herself a Jew, realized that she needed to do something. In fact, her cousin Mordecai suggested that for this cause she was made queen. First, she asked all the Jews to pray. And then, rather than barging in to see her husband, the king, and demanding that something be done about Haman, she invited him to a feast. At the feast, Esther made sure that she looked beautiful and that the food was great. And she didn't ask anything of the king except that he come back to another banquet. Timing is everything! At the second feast, the king asked Esther what her petition was. She asked him to spare her life, telling him that Haman was plotting to kill all the Jews, including herself. The king was outraged and had Haman killed, and then as king, he provided a way for the Jews to defend themselves.

Because Esther handled the situation in a respectful, honoring fashion, not only was her life saved, but the lives of thousands of Jews were spared. When you begin to demonstrate respect to

your husband, not only will he be changed, not only will the relationship be strengthened, but also you will be an example of how to love to all those watching.

Perhaps you are frustrated because you feel your husband doesn't deserve respect. Don't despair! Find one good thing he does (there should be at least one—after all, you did marry him), and honor him for that. Change how you speak to him, and I believe you will see the results.

When you demonstrate respect to him, he will accomplish great things.

dumb things she does #3

Trying to Fix Him

(Not That He Doesn't Need a Good Fixing!)

I could hardly wait to marry Philip for a few reasons (one of which had to do with having been celibate for a long time!). Another reason was that he needed some "fixing," and I was just the girl to do it. Most of us can hardly wait to marry the guys so that we can start changing them. We don't mean anything wrong by our attempts to change them; the relationship is just so important to us that we want to help it in whatever way possible.

John Gray, in his book *Men Are from Mars; Women Are from Venus,* says, "When we try to improve a man, he feels we are trying to fix him. The motto of most men is, 'If it's not broken, don't fix it.' So if we are trying to fix him, he is receiving the message that he is 'broken.'"

Then he starts acting "broken," which is not what you want! You

don't realize that your loving attempts to help him are really disrespectful. (Remember, feeling respected is his number one need.) You think that you are just helping him grow and that he is resisting your attempt to improve him. (Actually he calls it nagging.) You think he is unwilling to change. The truth is, he is resistant to changing because he believes he is not being respected. When a man feels respected, automatically he begins to grow.

Of course, there are changes you want him to make; yes, there are areas he needs to grow in, in order to be the ideal husband. However, you can be a help or a hindrance! Women have come to me frustrated because their husbands were not being the husbands they wanted. Sometimes, after listening to them for a while, I was not surprised. Daily they were telling their husbands what they needed to do and how they needed to do it. Men will shut down after hearing too much of this. Believe it or not, a man will change not as a result of how many times you say something, but as a result of your conduct and your quiet encouragement. It is hard for me to believe that sometimes by actually being quiet, I can accomplish more than with my many brilliant words, but that is the truth.

We all want our husbands to spend what we consider to be an appropriate amount of time with our children. What I've seen, however, is that while they are with the children, we offer all sorts

of "suggestions" about how they should do things. When our son, Jordan, was young, my husband offered to stay with him while I ran some errands. When I got back, I noticed the diaper was on backward—the little tape tabs were in the back. I quickly pointed this out to my husband and gave him an unasked-for diapering lesson. As time passed, I noticed that Philip was not offering to change Jordan's diaper very much. I realized what I had done and began to back off. Really, what does it matter if the diaper is on backward or upside down, as long as it's doing its job? And so what if Dad feeds the children junk food the night he's got them? Let him be the dad and spend time with them the way he wants.

A friend complained to me that when her husband did the laundry, he put the towels and the sheets in the same load (as if that were a major crime). I would be excited if my husband knew where the washing machine was! I suggested to her that if she ever wanted him to do laundry again, she shouldn't complain, but encourage and be grateful.

I am not quite sure how my husband managed to drive himself around for thirty-one years before he met me. Once we were married, I began to "fix" his driving, telling him what streets to take, the quickest way to get somewhere, and stomping my foot on the invisible brake pedal on my side of the car whenever he got too close to another car. When I began to grow in the area of showing respect

to my husband by not trying to fix him, it affected many areas of our life together. I knew I had to give up my backseat driving. (I was actually allowed to sit in the front seat after a while!) I also knew it would be tough.

One day we were coming home from church on a route we had traveled hundreds of times. This time, I was determined to be silent, no matter how hard it was. Sure enough, as we came up to the freeway's off-ramp where we needed to exit, my husband sailed right on past it. I bit my tongue as we drove and drove and drove miles past our destination. Finally Philip snapped out of whatever dazed state he had been in and asked, "Where in the world are we?"

I calmly said, "Woodland Hills" (which was the next town from ours). We both laughed, but I learned a valuable lesson. (Philip did too.) He frequently asks me to help in finding a certain location, but I now do it with an entirely different attitude.

A man doesn't usually leave his wife for someone prettier or for someone with more money, but for some woman who respects him, some woman who thinks he "hung the moon." I remember talking to a woman whose husband had just left her. (This obviously was not the best choice for him to make.) She was complaining that he had left her for "some bimbo who thinks he's just wonderful." She proudly told me that *she* hadn't seen him through rose-colored glasses; *she* had stood up to him and had challenged

him often. She hadn't seen him as some sort of superhero, as his new girlfriend did. I felt bad for her because her pride was going to be a lonely companion in the years to come. Men need to feel respected. Your husband is looking to be someone's hero. Why not let him be yours?

Deep inside every man there is a hero or knight in shining armor. More than anything, he wants to succeed in serving and protecting the woman he loves. When he feels trusted, he is able to tap into this noble part of himself. He becomes more caring. When he doesn't feel trusted, he loses some of his aliveness and energy, and after a while, he can stop caring.

Imagine a knight in shining armor traveling through the countryside. Suddenly he hears a woman crying out in distress. In an instant he comes alive. Urging his horse to a gallop, he races to her castle, where a dragon traps her. The noble knight pulls out his sword and slays the dragon.

As the gates open, he is welcomed and celebrated by the family of the princess and the townspeople. He is invited to live in the town and is acknowledged as a hero. He and the princess fall in love.

A month later, the noble knight goes off on another trip. On his way back, he hears his beloved princess crying out for help. Another dragon has attacked the castle. When the knight arrives, he pulls out his sword to slay the dragon.

Before he swings, the princess cries out from the tower, "Don't use your sword; use this noose. It will work better." She throws him the noose and

motions to him instructions about how to use it. He hesitantly follows her instructions. The dragon dies and everyone rejoices.

At the celebration dinner, the knight feels he didn't really do anything. Somehow, because he used her noose and didn't use his sword, he doesn't quite feel worthy of the town's trust and admiration. After the event, he is slightly depressed and forgets to shine his armor.

A month later, he goes on yet another trip. As he leaves with his sword, the princess reminds him to be careful and tells him to take the noose. On his way home, he sees yet another dragon attacking the castle. This time he rushes forward with his sword but hesitates, thinking maybe he should use the noose. In that moment of hesitation, the dragon breathes fire and burns his right arm. In confusion, he looks up and sees his princess waving from the castle window. "Use the poison," she yells. "The noose doesn't work."

She throws him the poison, which he pours into the dragon's mouth, and the dragon dies. Everyone rejoices and celebrates, but the knight feels ashamed.

A month later, he goes on another trip. As he leaves with his sword, the princess reminds him to be careful and to take the noose and the poison. He is annoyed by her suggestions but takes them just in case.

This time on his journey he hears another woman in distress. As he rushes to her call, his depression is lifted, and he feels confident and alive. But as he draws his sword to slay the dragon, he again hesitates. He wonders,

Trying to Fix Him

Should I use my sword, the noose, or the poison? What would the princess say?

For a moment he is confused. But then he remembers how he had felt before he knew the princess, back in the days when he carried only a sword. With a burst of renewed confidence he throws off the noose and poison, and charges the dragon with his trusted sword. He slays the dragon and the townspeople rejoice.

The knight in shining armor never returned to his princess. He stayed in this new village and lived happily ever after. He eventually married, but only after making sure his new partner knew nothing about nooses and poisons.

Remembering that within every man is a knight in shining armor is a powerful metaphor to help you remember a man's primary needs. Although a man may appreciate caring and assistance, sometimes too much of it will lessen his confidence or turn him off. (*Men Are from Mars, Women Are from Venus,* p. 138)

Your job is not to fix or change your husband. You are not his teacher, although there are times when he will learn from you. You are to be the influence, letting your heart, character, and integrity speak for themselves.

Come on, women, we can do this! Find a girlfriend who is also committed to respecting her husband as you are, and encourage each other. Help each other in your pursuit of a wonderful marriage.

There are plenty of things in your life to fix; your husband is not one of them.

dumb things she does #4

Not Getting Involved in What He's Doing

(He Really Does Want You There!)

It is good for each of us to have our own interests. In fact, it is very important. Although my husband is a huge part of my life, he is not the only part. That's too much pressure to put on anyone. I should have my own friends, my own interests, and my own goals that all contribute to making me a fun and interesting person. And at the same time, I can't be so busy with "my life" that Philip and I become separate, each doing his or her own thing. We need to share some areas of life.

My husband is a pastor, and when I met him, I knew that he wanted to be a pastor, although he hadn't started the church yet. When we made the decision to get married, he assured me that he didn't have any preconceived ideas about what a pastor's wife should do. He said that he just wanted me to be *his* wife and that

my role would eventually become evident. He wasn't expecting me to play the piano or sing (good thing!), which is what I thought was the traditional role of a pastor's wife. So, when we first started in the church, I volunteered in many areas, but was always focused on discovering the place I really felt comfortable in. As I grew and the purpose for my life became clearer, I began to work alongside my husband. I began teaching more and more, and we truly began to share more of the load. Teaching isn't necessarily the role every pastor's wife should fill, but it was a role suited for me. We now share the work and the vision of the ministry.

If your husband is an auto mechanic, you don't necessarily need to know how to fix a car (thank God!), but you should know something about what he does. If your husband is a computer designer or technician, you don't have to understand everything about computers (I certainly don't!), but you should respect his job enough to be able to carry on a conversation, using some computer language. If your husband is a physician or an attorney and belongs to various associations, attend some meetings and functions with him. Find some way to share his job with him, even though you don't have the same job.

Sharing some of the same interests is also important. Philip really likes basketball. Before I met him, I knew what a basketball looked like and the difference between offense and defense, but that was about it (despite the fact that I began my college career at Duke

University, which is a big basketball school). Rather than resent the fact that my husband is a basketball maniac, I decided to join him. I now go to the games with him, and I actually cheer much louder than he does. I know many of the players, what teams are doing well, and a lot of the basketball lingo. I knew I had it really bad when during the basketball play-offs, I had the game on the television and Philip wasn't even home!

What is your husband involved in? What is one of his interests that you can share, at least on some level? Read some of the same books. The kinds of books that Philip likes aren't necessarily my favorite, but I read some of them. We have great discussions, and my willingness to do this demonstrates to him that I am interested in him, what he thinks and what he does. At the same time, over the years, he has shown interest in my pursuits and desires. (Like sitting through romantic, girl-type movies with me—not just once either!) Although each of us has different interests that make us who we are, we benefit by finding areas that we can share.

Share the work, and share the fun.

dumb things she does #5

Being a Dream Stealer

(C'mon, Pull Out Those Pom-Poms and Cheer Him On!)

Most people, including your husband, are surrounded by negativity all day. Some of the negativity comes from outside influences, but some comes from inside, springing up from his self-doubts. He can be bombarded with comments such as, "That'll never work!" "No, I can't do that." "I don't have what it takes." "I'm not qualified to do this." You need to be his encourager, the one who says, "You *can* do it! What a great idea!"

I was a cheerleader in high school. Now, the social ramifications that go with that position today might not be so great, but the honor of being someone's cheerleader is. You should be your husband's cheerleader! He needs it, and he won't get it from most other people. A cheerleader is someone who speaks encouragement.

The word *encourage* means "to put courage in." Courage means

facing danger in spite of fear. As we encourage, we are saying, "Keep going; keep doing right; you'll get it!" When my son was ten months old, he decided he was ready to walk. I propped him up against a wall, and my husband was ready with the video camera. My son took one little step and then fell on his rear end. I cheered loudly, clapping and telling him what a great job he did. I stood him back up, and he began the process again. He took a few faltering steps before he fell. I hugged him, told him how smart he was, and we started again. Now, did I want him to walk like that forever? No. I was actually hoping that, sooner or later, he could string more than two wobbly steps together. But in the meantime, I encouraged every step he made.

As wives, we need to encourage every step our husbands take in the right direction. Your husband may not be doing something exactly how you want him to, but encourage him along the way. If he is reading books about, and generally working on, his relationship with you, encourage any good thing you see. Instead of complaining about the kind of flowers he brought, thank him! When he says he's coming home early, and it's not as early as you'd hoped for, don't attack him for it as soon as he walks in the door! Be thankful and enjoy the extra time together.

Avoid being critical and impatient, expecting him to get it right immediately. You and I don't always get it right either, so let's dish out

the encouragement that we ourselves need. How many of us have ever made a mistake? All of us. Wouldn't it be great if our spouses were cheering us on as we picked ourselves up and started again?

Applaud his dreams and his attempts to reach them.

dumb things she does #6

Not Understanding Your Role

(Take a Deep Breath Before Reading This One!)

Believe it or not, there was a time in history when women were considered to be of less value than oxen. Over time, the pendulum swung until we, as women, were told we had to be like men to succeed. The truth is in neither position. I am definitely of more value than an ox, and I don't have to be a man, think like a man (really, who could?), act like a man, or assume a man's role to fulfill my destiny. So what exactly is the role of the woman, especially in marriage?

Throughout history the husband has traditionally been in a leadership role in the family, and the wife in the helper role, submitted, if you will, to the husband's position. What does this mean to me and you today?

Author P. B. Wilson, in an appearance on *Oprah,* talked about her

book *Liberated Through Submission.* Oprah asked what *submission* meant, and the author responded that *submission* means what the dictionary says it means. It means "to yield" . . . to people, precepts, and principles that have been placed in our lives as authorities. She went on to explain that throughout our lives someone is always in authority, whether it be our parents, a teacher, an employer, or the president of our country.

She then proceeded to paint a picture of what submission looks like by asking us to imagine that there are two vehicles traveling down a freeway. On the right is a semi-trailer, and on the left, a compact car. The vehicles travel side by side for fifteen minutes or so, and then a sign appears indicating that the two lanes must merge into one. Based on the *position* of the truck, it has to yield to the compact car. The semi is stronger, bigger, and more powerful. It could force its way. But if it did, there would be a collision. And so the semi yields to the compact car, and they progressively move down the freeway until the lanes open up and they are side by side once again. I thought this to be an interesting picture.

Another way to look at submission is the team concept. On a sports team, there is just one head coach. Imagine the confusion on the team if more than one person were giving the players direction. The coach certainly isn't more important than the players. He just has a different *position.* His job is to recognize the strengths of the

different players and to let them do their stuff. When Phil Jackson was head coach of the Chicago Bulls, his job was to utilize the strengths of Michael Jordan, Scottie Pippin, and Dennis Rodman and to direct them to work together. He did not try to control Dennis Rodman (who could?) or turn him into another Michael Jordan. He recognized the defensive strengths of Rodman and encouraged them. His job of creating a championship team was made easier as the players yielded, or submitted, to his direction. Because Phil Jackson had earned his players' trust, Michael Jordan had no trouble submitting to his coach's leadership.

When I was in my twenties and heard the word *submission,* it would make me cringe. It was like fingernails being run down a chalkboard. Aagh! I was raised, probably like many of you, in a generation that was encouraged to challenge authority and submit to no one. Helen Reddy sang, "I am woman, hear me roar," and it was an appropriate theme song. The feminists were telling me, a well-educated, well-traveled woman, to focus on a chosen career and not to let a family or husband cloud the way. I was encouraged to believe that a career would meet most of my needs. If I still wanted a family, I could do that later; there was always time.

Although I am grateful for the benefits brought about by the feminists in the workplace and in society, they did not teach me accurately about how to relate to a man and be a part of a husband-wife

team. I didn't learn that my family should be my number one priority in order for it to be a successful one.

As a married woman, I was trying to figure out my role in the marriage. I knew it had to be somewhat different from Philip's so that each of us could bring strengths to the relationship. There had to be a way to make it work, and I set out to find it. I had seen too many marriages blow apart because both the husband and the wife were striving to be in charge—neither yielding to the other. I had also seen marriages dissolve because the husband had some weird concept in his mind that his wife should submit to his control and be dominated. The wife didn't take that for very long.

Listening to author P. B. Wilson talk about submission, I didn't like what I heard at first. However, I did see how submission was crucial in society, in the workplace, and in government. Some of you are employers and probably good ones who value your employees. Your employees are not inferior to you; they just have a different position and role. Are they less valuable? No. Could you do your job as well without them? No. Do you want your employees fighting for your position? Probably not. You want them to offer input and suggestions, but ultimately you want them to submit to your leadership as the boss. If you are an employee, your job is to support your boss, regardless of whether you are male or female.

Not Understanding Your Role

I met Shanelle about ten years ago while she was attending the University of Southern California. A very intelligent woman, she soon graduated with an engineering degree. After she had been working for a few months at her first job, which she had been thrilled to get, she came to me complaining about her boss. She claimed that she knew more than he did. He was too hard to work for and didn't listen to her ideas. He never admitted when he was wrong, which was often, nor did he give her credit for good ideas she had come up with. She didn't think she could take it anymore. I agreed with her that it sounded like a difficult situation, and then asked her if she wanted some help in dealing with it. She replied, "Yes." Our conversation basically went something like this:

"Shanelle, do you believe this is the job that will use your skills effectively?"

"Yes."

"Are there still things you can learn from this company?"

"Yes."

"What do you think your job as an employee is?"

"I guess it's to do the work I am asked to do and do it well."

"Are you doing that?"

"Well, my boss makes it so hard!"

"Who said life was easy? Your job as his employee is to learn from him, to be a good representative of him, to adapt yourself to

his requirements, and to be faithful to do good work . . . that is, if you want a promotion."

She assured me that she did want to advance in the company and that she was willing to make some changes in her attitude. It wasn't an easy task, but she began to yield to her boss and be supportive. She quit complaining about him and began to do the work he asked without having an "I know better" attitude (and in many instances she did know better; that was what made it a real challenge!). In a short span of years, she was promoted to the vice-president level of her company, where she was the highest-paid woman executive. At every level along the way people saw how hard she worked, no matter who her boss was, and so they kept promoting her. She even bypassed her initial boss.

Shanelle was promoted time and again over other men and women who didn't understand this concept. She wasn't a doormat. She ex-pressed her opinions whenever they were requested. She was promoted over men and women who were trying to fight their way to the top, complaining about their bosses all the way. She learned to respect her boss's position, whether she ever respected the person as an individual. She continued to find favor within the company and with her clients all over the world. Now, I believe, as a direct result of her understanding this concept, she was offered and accepted a position as an officer in the United Nations, where

she has had global influence. She went from being a frustrated low-level engineer to one of the most influential women in an organization of worldwide importance, spending her time with presidents and heads of state.

As a citizen of the United States, I am submitted to the government of our country and its president. Do I necessarily agree with him and the decisions he makes? No, but I must still submit to the *position* of the presidency. I pay taxes and stop at red lights (well, most of them!) because I am submitted to the laws in my country. The motto for the state of Kentucky is "United we stand, divided we fall." This is true for any company, my country, and my marriage. In marriage I believe that as wives, we are to yield to the *position* of the husband. Now before you start yelling, let me explain what I mean. (If you still want to yell at the end, go ahead.)

Over time I began to see the value in there being just one head in a marriage (a two-headed anything is a monster). If my husband is the "coach," then I am his star player. (I think I'm going to ask for a raise!) Perhaps some of you are shuddering at this picture. Why? Why do we scorn submission? Maybe we can picture only the horror of being controlled or abused. Let me make this clear. *No* human being has the right to dominate, control, or abuse another. No matter what. We need to make a paradigm shift because I believe what we have always assumed about submission is not accurate.

- Submission is *not* yielding to abuse. If you are in an abusive relationship, get out and get help.
- Submission is *not* being subservient.
- Submission is *not* being a mousy doormat.
- Submission is *not* keeping your mouth shut at all costs.
- Submission is *not* doing whatever you are asked to do even if you are uncomfortable with it.
- Submission is *not* yielding to foolishness or ignorance.

One of the definitions of *submission* is "to make yourself adaptable." Can you adapt yourself so that the team succeeds? It takes a strong woman to do that, one who isn't afraid she's going to lose her own identity. I believe the majority of us have had a hard time being adaptable—either at home or at work—because we are concerned that our strengths won't be recognized, or because we'll lose our individual identity.

Another definition is "to be cooperative." I would like to suggest that for any relationship to succeed the *we* has to become more important than the *me*. Cooperation is the key. It can't be "my way" or "your way"; instead it should be "our way." My marriage, as a unit, is more important than either my individual needs and wants or Philip's individual desires. In a marriage, submission

works *only* because the husband has earned the trust of the wife, not because he is more demanding than she is.

The truth is, Philip and I have learned to submit to each other. There are times when he yields to my strengths. In a room full of strangers, I am more outgoing than he is, and so in those situations, I take the lead and we make lots of new friends. Math comes easy for me; therefore, I usually am the one doing anything math-related. Because Philip is confident in who he is, he is not afraid or threatened by my strengths, but encourages them. Just as there were times when Coach Phil Jackson said, "Michael, take the ball and do your thing." He wasn't afraid of Michael's strengths, and Michael didn't try to become coach. I recognize that there are men who are not confident in themselves and so attempt to dominate and control. I talk to them in the other section.

Although there is no guarantee of a man's response, here's a suggestion on how to handle a typical scenario.

"My husband is an idiot at handling the finances. Am I supposed to submit to his ignorance and let him mess us up financially?"

No. Begin a conversation, without attacking, and say something like this:

"Honey, how about if I handle the finances? We'll talk after a month and see if you like what I've done. Because what I'd like to do is strengthen our situation, and you have enough on your plate."

In the previous chapters I have covered topics such as respecting your husband and talking to him in a way that demonstrates that. I have mentioned that trying to fix your husband is not a good idea. And I have talked about the importance of involving yourself in some areas of his life as well as being his number one cheerleader. If you can do these things, you are adapting yourself to him and being cooperative, honoring the relationship more than your own comfort zone. Good for you! Wouldn't our world be a pleasant place to live in if we were all committed to honoring each other and not being so self-centered?

I have seen bumper stickers that say, "Practice random acts of kindness." What a great world it would be if we all actually did that. Submitting, or being adaptable and cooperative, means being kind, deferring to the other, letting them go first, be right, win, get the recognition—whatever—and is something all men and women should become good at. We can do this because we are confident in who we are and we are not afraid to give.

If you still feel like yelling, go ahead. You certainly don't have to agree with me. One woman I spoke with on a radio show was having quite a hard time with this idea, and yet was in regular conflict with her husband about decisions. I suggested that she give the concept a try; maybe they could alternate days of who had the final say in a decision. Or perhaps, depending on the subject in discussion,

the one who had experience in that particular area could be the final decision maker. Something needed to change in order for there to be peace in their home. Two people fighting to be the decision maker makes for a very unpleasant home.

I found that this concept works in my marriage, and I have grown and become stronger because of it. If you are married, ask your husband what he thinks. If you are in a relationship, ask the man you are dating. If nothing else, this will provide interesting fodder for a conversation!

Try being adaptable and flexible.
See what happens!

One Last Thing

(And I Do Mean That!)

Thanks for taking the time to read my little book. I hope that the title of this book is not offensive to anyone. I am certainly not saying that any one of you is dumb! However, most of us have done at least one or two dumb things in our lives.

My desire is that you will take whatever you learned in these pages and put it to use in your marriage and your relationships. And I hope that you will continue to read books on men, women, and marriage. Many wonderful books out there can help take your relationship to the next level.

And please take the time to include God in your marriage. There have been countless studies done and numerous polls taken around the world that prove that allowing God into your relationship is

amazingly beneficial. Spend time together praying. Perhaps you've seen the billboards that say, "The family that prays together stays together." I agree. When God is on the scene, there are joy, peace, and love. What relationship could survive without those?

I'll leave you with a thought from Howard Whitman: "It takes guts to stay married . . . There will be many crises between the wedding day and the golden anniversary, and the people who make it are heroes" (*Philadelphia Sunday Bulletin,* January 15, 1967).

So, go on, get out there, and build the strongest relationship possible.

The dumbest thing we could do is read a book like this and do nothing about it!

About the Author

Holly Wagner is a popular speaker at conferences around the world, from Los Angeles to Australia, New Zealand, Canada, Scotland, and Wales. She always makes an impact on her audiences and is known for her challenging, personable, and humorous style of addressing real life issues. While dealing with situations that are important to us

all, she gives powerful and tremendously impacting direction in the area of building friendships, enhancing marriages, and character development.

Crowned Miss Texas National Teenager at the age of eighteen, Holly went on to attend Duke University and Southern Methodist University. She then moved to Los Angeles working as an actress in TV, film, and modeling. Holly has appeared on television's *Fox Family Channel*, *The 700 Club*, *100 Huntley Street*, *On Main Street*, *Good Morning Sydney*, the Australian *Beauty and the Beast* and *Good Morning Australia* speaking on effective relationships.

Her husband, Philip, is the Senior Pastor of The Oasis Christian Center, in Los Angeles, and together they lead this unique multiracial church that reaches the entertainers of Hollywood, families, and the business leaders in the community. Holly is one of the main teachers in the church and leads a dynamic women's ministry, encouraging women to be who God called them to be.

Holly loves all the parts of her life! She loves being Philip's wife and working on her marriage. She has a great time with her two children, Jordan and Paris, and is often seen cheering for their baseball and basketball teams! For recreation, she enjoys spending time with her family and friends. She likes to exercise, having earned a black belt in karate, and goes scuba diving with her husband in some of the most beautiful spots in the world!